BILLY TWINKLE
REQUIEM FOR A GOLDEN BOY

Other books by Ronnie Burkett:

STRING QUARTET
TINKA'S NEW DRESS
STREET OF BLOOD
HAPPY
PROVENANCE

10 DAYS ON EARTH

BILLY TWINKLE

TWINKLE

REQUIEM FOR A GOLDEN BOY

BY RONNIE BURKETT

Playwrights Canada Press
Toronto • Canada

Billy Twinkle: Requiem for a Golden Boy © Copyright 2008 Ronnie Burkett

PLAYWRIGHTS CANADA PRESS
The Canadian Drama Publisher
215 Spadina Ave., Suite 230, Toronto, ON Canada M5T 2C7
phone 416.703.0013   fax 416.408.3402
orders@playwrightscanada.com • www.playwrightscanada.com

For professional or amateur production rights, please contact
John Lambert & Assoc. Inc.
2141 Boul. St-Joseph E. Montréal, Québec H2H 1E6
phone 514.982.6825   fax 514.982.6118   info@johnlambert.ca

The publisher acknowledges the support of the Canadian taxpayers through
the Government of Canada Book Publishing Industry Development Program,
the Canada Council for the Arts, the Ontario Arts Council,
and the Ontario Media Development Corporation.

Cover photos by Trudie Lee
Cover design by Blake Sproule
Typesetting: JLArt

Library and Archives Canada Cataloguing in Publication

Burkett, Ronnie, 1957–
Billy Twinkle : requiem for a golden boy / Ronnie Burkett.

A play.
ISBN 978-0-88754-885-7

I. Title.

PS8553.U639B54 2009   C812'.6   C2009-904745-4

First edition: December 2009
Printed and bound in Canada by Canadian Printco, Scarborough

*For the other little boys who grew up to be real live puppeteers,
and who, as adults, became my friends.
And in memory of the grand old men of puppetry
who paved the road before us;
especially Steve, who had the map and showed me the way.*

NOTES ON STAGING

The set for *Billy Twinkle* is a front-on view of a cruise ship. The set is elevated two feet above the theatre stage and floats on exposed steel struts atop a stylized painted-ocean floor. The main acting area is a wooden-plank deck with a pointed bow. Much of the action of the "human" Billy takes place on this deck, including each of his four "Stars in Miniature" variety acts. Flanking this are two curved floating staircases leading to the ship's bridge. The term bridge is also a standard puppetry term referring to the elevated platform in a traditional marionette theatre on which the puppeteer stands.

Below the bridge—and upstage of the central deck—is a small raised stage. At the beginning of the play, the area directly behind this stage is covered with a silver-tinsel Mylar curtain. This serves as the backdrop for Billy's variety numbers. The silver curtain parts in the middle and behind it is the puppet stage proscenium, which creates the acting area for all of the marionette flashback scenes throughout the play.

The proscenium arch features relief sculptures of all the characters in the play in a faux gold-leaf finish. The proscenium has a functioning red-velvet theatrical drape, which is opened and closed from the bridge above. Behind the proscenium is a curved cyclorama that is lit from underneath the stage and changes colour and pattern throughout the marionette scenes. The marionettes enter from alleys on each side of the puppet stage area, and are hung across the width of the stage at the back of the set when not in use.

The marionettes are long-strung at a floor-to-control height of ninety inches. Several characters are represented by a number of duplicate marionettes; to facilitate costume changes and different ages, Billy is represented by eight marionettes. Billy's variety act marionettes are short-strung in a typical cabaret style and are manipulated by Ronnie-as-Billy in full view. Several marionettes hold and control miniature marionettes of their own, creating a puppet show within a puppet show within a puppet show.

Stage directions herein are kept to a minimum. Standard staging abbreviations are used in this text, USC meaning "upstage centre," SL meaning "stage left" and so on. John Alcorn's score and Kevin Humphrey's lighting design are integral to the overall design and performance, although lighting and sound notes within this text are referred to only when necessary to the reading.

The play is performed without an interval, with a running time of approximately one hour and forty-seven minutes.

The original production of *Billy Twinkle: Requiem for a Golden Boy* was commissioned by the Citadel Theatre (Edmonton, Canada) and co-commissioned by Canada's National Arts Centre (Ottawa, Canada), the Vancouver East Cultural Centre (Vancouver, Canada), the Arts Centre (Melbourne, Australia), Sydney Opera House (Sydney, Australia), and the Barbican Centre BITE:09 (London, UK).

Billy Twinkle premiered at the Citadel Theatre, Edmonton, Alberta on October 23, 2008 with the following cast and crew:

Written and Performed by Ronnie Burkett
Marionette, Costume, and Set Design by Ronnie Burkett
Music and Sound Design by John Alcorn
Lighting Design by Kevin Humphrey
Production Manager / Artistic Associate: Terri Gillis
Technical Director: Shanna Miller
Stage Manager: Lesley Humphrey
Dramaturge: Iris Turcott
Associate Producer: John Lambert
Tour Administrator: Claire Chouinard

Produced by Rink-A-Dink Inc./Ronnie Burkett Theatre of Marionettes.

All production photographs by Trudie Lee.

Puppet Studio

Marionettes built by Ronnie Burkett
Head puppet builder: Dina Meschkuleit
Miniature marionettes by Angela Talbot
Additional character sculpture: Erik Schaper
Puppet builders: Gemma James-Smith, Robin Fisher, Ken MacKenzie
Additional assistance: Martin Herbert, Alexis Taylor
Costumes built by Kim Crossley, assisted by Gina Schellenberg and Anna Baines
Puppet animations by Mark Keetch
Controls and stringing: Luman Coad

Scene Shop

Head Scenic Carpenter: Les Myhr
Assistant Head Scenic Carpenter: Peter Locock
Scenic Carpenters: Chris Hayes and Kelly Menard
Head Scenic Artist: Michelle Dias

Music

Music and lyrics, arrangements and recording production by John Alcorn
Lyrics for "Word of Jesus Christ" by Ronnie Burkett
Additional orchestrations arranged and conducted by John MacLeod
Recording and mixing by Jeff Wolpert at Kick Audio and Desert Fish, Toronto

MUSICIANS

John Alcorn: piano, kazoo
Terry Clarke: drums
Bob DeAngelis: baritone saxophone, clarinet
Moshe Hammer: violin
John Johnson: alto saxophone, piccolo
Alastair Kay: trombone
Jason Logue: trumpet
John MacLeod: trumpet
Colin Murray: bass trombone
Reg Schwager: electric and nylon guitars
Don Thompson: piano, vibraphone
Steve Wallace: bass
Perry White: tenor saxophone, flute, recorder
Singers: Coco Love Alcorn, John Alcorn
Voiceovers: Gemma James-Smith, Frank Meschkuleit

SPECIAL THANKS

Rene Zendejas, Phillip Huber, Tony Urbano, Noreen Young, Eileen Burkett, Frank and Dina Meschkuleit, Lower Ossington Theatre, Eloisa Slimmon-Weber/Liberty Movement Studio, Karen Chapelle, Gary Busk, Michael Pearl/Liberty Market Building, Mary Adachi, and especially Bob Baker, Penny Ritco, and the staff of the Citadel Theatre.

CHARACTERS

BILLY TWINKLE, a mid-life cruise-ship puppeteer
RUSTY, a burlesque goddess
BUMBLEBEAR, a roller-skating animal act
SID DIAMOND, ghost, handpuppet, and Billy's mentor
PEGGY RUGGLES, Billy's mother
KEN RUGGLES, Billy's father
BENJI, another awkward puppeteer
BETTY BOBBY, singing teacher
RANDI RIVERS, a wronged woman of song
THE MAN, a travelling businessman
BIDDY BANTAM BREWSTER, society hostess
PETROOSTER, Petruchio anthropomorphized
COWTRINA, Kate as a cow
LESLEY KAYE, an elderly puppeteer
JULIET, post-Romeo
BRIAN, Billy's significant other
BUNNY, a senior with bunny ears
DOREEN GRAY, evangelist puppeteer
ROCKET, possibly the future

BILLY TWINKLE

REQUIEM FOR A GOLDEN BOY

*As the audience enters, the stage is lit in a dim
nighttime state. The set is a stylized front-on view
of a cruise ship, indicated by decking twenty-four
inches above the stage floor that forms a point, or
bow, downstage. Upstage centre, flanking the widest
part of the deck, are two sets of curved stairs leading
to a central bridge above the deck. At this level,
a waist-high leaning rail supports a silver Mylar
curtain on a track, which hits the floor and spans the
area between the two sets of stairs. Behind the bridge
is a rail holding most of the marionettes used in the
show, except for five, which are hung under the
stairs.*

*As house lights dim to half, music begins. It is, for
lack of a better word, "twinkly" with an angelic voice
singing BILLY's name. BILLY's show music begins
with an unseen announcer's introduction as the
house and stage go to black.*

ANNOUNCER   *(voice-over)* Ladies and gentlemen, Happy Sea Fun
Cruises proudly presents Mr. Billy Twinkle and his
Stars in Miniature!

*Music builds into a lush, Vegas-style full
orchestration intro of BILLY's theme. Lights up,
similarly all glitz and pizzazz. BILLY Twinkle stands
in front of the Mylar curtain in a pseudo-Fosse pose.
As the light shifts to a front-on, full-body spot, we see
that he looks fabulous. Showbiz fabulous, that is, in
a tuxedo with a blue-and-white striped sailor shirt
underneath. He is holding a marionette of an
elegant showgirl in a full-length gown and fur stole.*

*BILLY begins what is, to those in the know, a classic
marionette stripper routine, more reminiscent of
burlesque than of a modern stripper.*

There is no bump or grind here, this is one of those "classy" strip numbers; slow, tantalizing, and languid. The musical accompaniment is sexy and punctuates the strip.

The first article of clothing to be removed is the white fur stole, followed by the entire gown, which reveals a lace corset. When this is removed, the marionette is down to her bra and G-string. As the choreographed routine builds to its finish, she drops her bra and winks over her shoulder at the audience. Music finishes with a flourish. The spot snaps out and BILLY puts the puppet away under the stairs. Light restores on stage as BILLY addresses the audience.

BILLY Thank you. You're very kind, thank you. Whew, is it hot in here or was it just that last act? That, of course, was Miss Rusty Knockers. And, as is the custom here on Happy Seas Fun Cruises, I'll be bringing Rusty out after the show if any of you gentlemen would like to have your picture taken with her. And now, ladies and gentleman, continuing on with Stars in Miniature, I would like to introduce you to a very old friend of mine. We've been in this business a long time together, but, he's still a little shy. So, help me if you will, and welcome to the stage, Bumblebear!

GRIN AND BEAR IT

The music begins again, although sweeter in tone; a circus lullaby theme, if such a thing were to exist. BILLY brings out BUMBLEBEAR. He is a tired-looking, snaggle-toothed old bear wearing a tutu and roller skates. The act begins slowly, with the bear wobbling hesitantly on his skates. He stops, bats his eyes, and waves at the audience. Eventually, BUMBLEBEAR starts skating. At some point in the act, BILLY starts talking; not to the audience, but about them. His smile never wanes, nor does the act itself suffer.

BILLY   Oh God, they're talkers tonight. Why do they have to talk; I'm busting my ass out here. Does this look easy? Gimme a break. Oh, I should have known. Look at her. Typical. Big hair, big mouth. God, why are boring people so loud? Keep smiling, Billy. Oh yeah, that's right, mister, I'm just a big faggot. Did you enjoy your five buffets today, you bloated breeder whale? They put laxatives in the food so fat assholes like you don't clog the ship's plumbing. Have another piece of cheesecake, shithead. Smile, Billy. Oh God, listen to her. Shut up. Shut. Up. Shhh!

BILLY has audibly and directly shushed someone in the audience. Instantly, the music stops and the spotlight on the bear snaps out. The stage is lit, although not in showbiz state.

I shushed someone in the audience.

Fuck that felt good.

BUMBLEBEAR is put away under the stairs. BILLY removes his jacket.

He stands downstage centre at the ship's bow in a more contained and sombre light. It is night and the stage floor around the thrust of the ship set is deep blue. Behind him stars twinkle on the backcloth. He exhales deeply, a softer, prolonged version of his shush.

Ssssshhhhhhhhhhh...

He spreads his arms wide and mimics a moment from the film Titanic.

I'm the queen of the world!

His moment of contrived ecstasy is short-lived.

Ssssshhhhhhhhhhh... iiiiiiiit.

They fired me.

Oh God.

WINGING A PRAYER

*There is no physical railing at the bow of the ship,
but we imagine there is. BILLY looks over it, then
around him, over again, and finally lifts his head up
toward the sky. He looks over the rail once again,
checks to see that no one is watching, and drops to
his knees. Awkwardly and self-consciously he begins
to pray.*

BILLY   Oh God, thank you for this day and all the blessings
I have received. Forgive me my trespasses, like shushing
that peroxide pig in the audience tonight, for I know
she is also one of your children. And a pig. Sorry, but
it's true. Forgive my evil ways and deeds, like wishing
the whole audience would choke on chicken bones
at the midnight buffet or have diarrhea so bad they
dehydrate themselves to death, for I know they are all
thy children too. And forgive this child of yours for his
weakness, because I'm going to jump off the edge of
this boat, okay God?

I know, I'm not supposed to… call it a boat. It's a ship.
That's the first thing they teach you. And dear God,
I don't care. I don't want to do this anymore anyway.

It's not been a bad life, God. It's been okay. So, thank
you, Father in Heaven, for the bounty of thine okay.
This isn't the worst time I've ever known, God no. The
worst is farting on stage and knowing they heard it.
The worst is having a puppet in each hand and horking
a phlegm ball onto yourself and watching it slide down
your lapel. The worst is still using a headshot from
nine years ago because you haven't saved enough
money for the facelift. The worst is not liking puppets
anymore. That's the worst, by far.

And yes, thank you for the blessing of being one of the
top-rated cruise-ship puppeteers in the world, dear
Father; which, while not exactly the asshole of show
business, is at least sort of the belly button, but I'm
tired of being a bear in a tutu who dances in a floating
cage for stupid people to poke at. Happy Sea Fun

Cruises? Oh c'mon, what's so happy about it? Look what they make me wear! I look like gay Popeye. I look like Moby's dick. I look like an inflatable mime. I look like Cirque de So Gay. I don't want to do this anymore!

I've been doing this my whole life. And where did it get me, huh God? I'm invisible. Middle-aged and not even at a crossroads. I'd kill for a crossroads right about now. I'm a performer and you're the only audience I've got left, God? So I'm walking the plank because there's no lifeboat. No floatation device. It's sink or swim, and I'm drowning... in nautical metaphors.

Life will never be as beautiful as I imagined it.

He looks up one last time.

In thy holy name, amen.

SLINGS AND ARROWS

BILLY stands and prepares himself for the jump. We hear SID's voice. (Note: for the duration of the play, whenever the voice or the handpuppet of SID talks, BILLY's mouth visibly moves with no attempt to hide the fact.)

SID   "To be, or not to be, that is the question:"

BILLY looks over both shoulders, then over the edge into the water below. Very slowly he looks upward, cocks his head, and shakes it. He composes himself and prepares to jump again.

"Whether 'tis nobler in the mind to suffer
The slings and arrows of outrageous fortune,
Or to take arms against a sea of troubles
And by opposing end them."

BILLY stumbles backward, falling to the ground. He lies on his stomach, inches his way toward the point of the bow, and cautiously looks over the edge. He slowly sits up and looks toward the sky.

BILLY	Hello? God? God, that's you, right?
	Hi, God.
	Look, if you don't want me to do this, then give me a sign.
	Beat. Nothing.
	Okay then. Thy will be done.
	BILLY awkwardly crosses himself as only a non-Catholic can and raises his arms above his head in a diving pose.
SID	"To die—to sleep, No more; and by a sleep to say we end The heart-ache and the thousand natural shocks That flesh is heir to: 'tis a consummation Devoutly to be wish'd."
	Again, BILLY's concentration is broken, although this time he is more annoyed than perplexed.
BILLY	Okay, that's not God. I know those words. I know that voice. Sid! Sidney? Sid, I know you're there, waiting in the light and all, but Sid, for once could you be patient and at least let me get into the light before you start talking to me again? Okay?
	Okay.
	He shakes himself out and takes a few short breaths, not unlike an athlete, or worse, an actor.
	Let's give this another try.
	He raises his arms to dive, when again he is interrupted by SID's voice.
SID	"To die, to sleep; To sleep, perchance to dream—ay, there's the rub:"
	BILLY clasps his hands over his mouth to stifle the voice. His eyes grow wide at the realization that he has been saying these things. He slowly moves his hands slightly below his mouth.
	"For in that sleep of death what dreams may come,"

He covers his mouth again, then quickly moves his hands as if to trick himself.

"When we have shuffled off this mortal coil,"

BILLY   Whoa. Sid, stop it. This isn't funny. Sid, you're freaking me out here.

SID responds as BILLY dashes up the SL stairs to the bridge where he stands centre, visible from the waist up.

SID   "Thus conscience does make cowards of us all
And thus the native hue of resolution
Is sicklied o'er with the pale cast of thought,
And enterprises of great pitch and moment
With this regard their currents turn awry
And lose the name of action."

BILLY   Shhhh! Okay, okay, Sid, I get it. Yeah, the whole look-at-me-whiny-Hamlet to-be-or-not-to-be, should-I-kill-myself-or-not speech, but c'mon, knock it off, okay? I'm gonna do this, Sid. Personally, I think it's kind of appropriate: burial at sea; just like my career, hey Sid? Like you always said, there's nothing special about me. So see, who would care if I be or not be? So I'm doing this, Sid, and you're gonna shut up about it. Please, just shut up! And stop it with the soliloquizing already, okay, because I'm not going to die with that pussy boy Hamlet on my lips, do you hear me? I fucking hate Shakespeare, Sid!

Steadying himself with one hand, BILLY puts a leg up on the bridge railing in preparation to hoist himself up and over. BILLY's other hand is momentarily unseen while he places it into a handpuppet of SID Diamond. SID is elderly, nattily dressed, albeit with a slight ghostly pallor, and wears a pair of pink fabric bunny ears atop his head. With a short, menacing musical sting, he appears suddenly at BILLY's side.

SID   I beg your pardon, sir? You're not even worthy to wipe the Bard's…

BILLY turns quickly and sees SID.

BILLY

Aaaagh!

He screams and scrambles halfway onto the bridge railing while calling upward. The handpuppet SID grabs BILLY and pulls.

SID

Hold it right there, Twinkletoes! God's not listening to you. Why do you think I'm here?

BILLY

To drag me to hell!

SID

Very dramatic, sir, but trust me, you haven't the depth of talent to play a heaven-and-hell scene. So knock it off and listen to me!

BILLY

No! I won't. I won't listen to you!

BILLY tries to cover his ears with his hands, one of which is obviously manipulating the handpuppet. He runs down the SR stairs to the main deck, SID in tow.

La la la la la la la la, I can't hear you!

SID pulls BILLY's ear and whispers into it.

SID

Oh yes you can, Billy Ruggles.

BILLY

How do you know that name? Who are you, demon?

SID

Jesus Christ!

BILLY

Really?

SID

No! I mean, Jesus Christ you're an asshole! Billy, you were right the first time. It's me. Sid!

BILLY

Liar! Demon! Devil! You're not Sid! Sid Diamond was a man. You're just a...

SID

Yes?

BILLY

A handpuppet with horns.

SID

They're not horns, Billy. Take a closer look.

The handpuppet grabs BILLY's face and turns it toward him. BILLY looks up at the ears.

BILLY	They're bunny ears.
	BILLY pulls away slowly from SID's hands.
	Sid?
	The handpuppet nods his head.
SID	Mmm hmm?
BILLY	Sid, why are you a handpuppet wearing bunny ears?
SID	I think you know the answer to that, Billy.
BILLY	No, how would I?
SID	Because this is your doing!
BILLY	I don't make handpuppets, Sid. Please, you know me better than that!
SID	Oh no, you were trained to make marionettes, weren't you, Billy? You were trained by me. But you were not trained to make a marionette of me wearing bunny ears for a comedy routine in your act, which is what you did after I died. And keeps me from being truly dead and crossing over into the light! Don't mess with that shit, Billy! Do you have any idea what it's like being stuck in the middle?
BILLY	Yes, Sid, I do! That's why I'm going to die.
SID	Oh no you're not! If anyone's dying around here, it's me!
BILLY	You're already dead!
SID	Half-dead!
BILLY	Whatever.
SID	I'm here to see that you retire that old man with the bunny ears routine and make things right so I can cross into the light.
BILLY	I was minding my own business, just trying to kill myself, when you barged in. So if you don't mind, Sid, I'd like to get back to what I was doing and end my life.

SID   You don't get to end your life, Billy, but you have to finish it. And I'm here to see that you do.

BILLY   And what if I don't want to?

SID   Boo hoo. Who cares what you want? It's what you need.

BILLY   What I need, Sid, is for you to fuck off!

SID   "O villain, villain, smiling, damned villain!"

> They fight. SID grabs BILLY's throat, and as BILLY tries to fend off the handpuppet, they thrash about the deck. BILLY is thrown to the floor, his head DSC at the point of the bow, with SID sitting on his chest.

Now will you listen to me?

BILLY   No, I won't, because you're not going to talk anymore.

SID   Sir, I've just begun!

BILLY   No, you're done. You've been using my mouth, Sid. What the hell is that about?

SID   Gee, I don't know. I'm a puppet and you're a puppeteer. Figure it out, asshole!

BILLY   Well too bad, Sid. This mouth is closed for business.

SID   That mouth has never been closed for business. Faggot.

BILLY   Suck this, handpuppet!

> BILLY sits up quickly, grabs the back of SID's head, and forces it down onto his crotch. SID screams and his cries continue as BILLY holds his head firmly. SID's resistance turns into a muffled, plaintive whimper.

Had enough?

SID   Mmmm hmmm.

BILLY   Will you behave yourself?

SID   Mmmm hmmm.

BILLY   No more talking?

SID   Uh uh.

BILLY	Fine. Now, let me die in peace.

> *BILLY releases SID's head, who instantly jumps up. SID leaps at BILLY and they fight again. It's a fast, down-and-out brawl as each spews Shakespeare.*

SID	"To-morrow, and to-morrow, and to-morrow, Creeps in this petty pace from day to day, To the last syllable of recorded time; And all our yesterdays have lighted fools The way to dusty death."
BILLY	"Out, out, brief candle! Life's but a walking shadow, a poor player, That struts and frets his hour upon the stage, And then is heard no more. It is a tale Told by an idiot, full of sound and fury, Signifying nothing."

> *They sit up, panting.*

SID	Not bad, although it was a bit overplayed for my taste.
BILLY	Yes, I remember your Macbeth, Sid.
SID	Don't say that name out loud! Not here. You know it's bad luck to say the M word in a theatre!
BILLY	Macbeth, Macbeth, Macbeth! We're not in a theatre, Sid.
SID	Then what do you call this?

> *BILLY's hand thrusts outward off the ship deck as SID jumps. BILLY's body follows, and he lands on the stage floor, writhing and gasping as if drowning in a pool of water. But there is no water, only stage. BILLY, confused, sits upright. SID has been watching this with folded arms, perched high on BILLY's upright left arm throughout the action.*

	See? I was right, again. It's a stage.
BILLY	But I was on a ship.
SID	"There are more things in heaven and earth, Horatio, Than are dreamt of in your philosophy."

Turn up the lights!

The house lights come up to half in the theatre, accompanied by a short musical sting.

See?

BILLY   Sid, who are those people? Is this heaven?

SID   Like hell! They're punters, The Great Unwashed, spectators, subscribers, devotees of Thespus, whatever you want to call them. They're your audience, kid!

BILLY   I got fired, Sid.

SID   New production! Starring… you! The Billy Twinkle Show. Your life, condensed and in miniature!

BILLY   What happened to life flashing before my eyes?

SID   Billy, life doesn't flash; it's acted out, line by line, scene by scene. Some are comedies, some not so, most are in-between.

SID leads BILLY back onto the deck.

Tell me, what have you always wanted more than anything?

BILLY thinks for a second and starts to open his mouth.

Besides a huge cock.

BILLY frowns somewhat, in a mixture of disapproval and disappointment. He thinks and is silent.

Well?

BILLY   I dunno.

SID   Oh come on, Billy, think!

BILLY   I got nothin', Sid.

SID   You can't be serious, sir!

BILLY   Sorry. You kind of had me on the cock thing.

A REAL LIVE BOY

*SID leads BILLY upstage in front of BILLY's show
curtain. SID moves to one side and starts to pull
a rope-and-pulley curtain rig.*

SID   Well, don't just stand there. Help me!

*BILLY helps SID with his one free hand and,
taking turns together on the overhand pull, open
the curtain to reveal a beautiful marionette theatre
proscenium. We hear BILLY's theme for the first
time and it plays through the reveal and under the
following action.*

Ta da! What you've always dreamed of, Billy. The most
beautiful marionette theatre in the world!

BILLY   Holy Lonely Goatherd!

SID   Give it a spin.

*BILLY, with SID in tow, climbs one of the side stairs
and stands on the bridge overlooking the marionette
stage. Turning, he notices all the marionettes
hanging US behind the marionette theatre.*

BILLY   Oh my God, look at all these puppets.

SID   Shall we have a jiggle? Wiggle the wood?

BILLY   I don't know what we're doing.

SID   But you've already done it, Billy. So, get a hold of
yourself and remember.

BILLY   Remember what, Sid?

SID   A real live boy who dreamed of being a puppeteer.

*BILLY walks a marionette from backstage into the
playing area below. It is BILLY, age eleven.*

BOHEMIAN RHAPSODIZING

Transition. Music in, a bouncy tune reminiscent of a 1960s children's television theme. As light shifts from the upper bridge area to the marionette theatre, the marionette of child BILLY stands on stage watching an unseen TV. SID is put away, hung upside down on the back of the bridge leaning rail. The curtains of the puppet theatre open and inside the cyclorama is awash with bright morning colour. As the transition settles, music has become the obvious audio of a children's television show, complete with recorded puppet voices, all with British accents.

PRINCESS   *(voice-over)* Oh Robin Woodmouse, I don't know how I can ever thank you!

ROBIN   *(voice-over)* No need for that, Princess Lillydew. Why, if your trusted servants Pippin and Posey hadn't found the evil wizard's lair, you'd still be in the soup!

They laugh.

PRINCESS   *(voice-over)* You're so right, Robin Woodmouse! Pippin, Posey, how can I ever thank you, my trusted fairy friends?

PIPPIN   *(voice-over)* Perhaps with grangleberry tea…

POSEY   *(voice-over)* Oh yes, and lovely little fern sugar cakes!

PRINCESS   *(voice-over)* Oh you two!

They all laugh again.

The theme music for the television show swells and concludes. PEGGY Ruggles, BILLY's mother, enters. She is dressed like an early 1960s working woman with cat's-eye glasses, a pencil skirt, fitted cardigan, and a simple strand of pearls.

PEGGY   Billy, turn that television set off this instant. You know there's no TV before school.

BILLY, 11   But it was *Teeny Tot Forest.*

PEGGY	Billy, how many eleven-year-old boys watch *Teeny Tot Forest*?
BILLY, 11	It's marionettes, Mum. And Robin Woodmouse has a moving mouth. I'm just watching so I can figure out how it's done.
PEGGY	Robin Woodmouse! I don't know why those British people think mice are so darn cute. One day here in Saskatchewan and they'd soon learn there's no reason to celebrate rodents. Ken! Let's move it, Mr. Ruggles. We have to drop Billy at school and I don't want to be late for work. Not today.
BILLY, 11	You look nice, Mum.
PEGGY	Do you think? Is it okay? Robert's coming to the Rexall today and we're having a luncheon meeting.
BILLY, 11	Who's Robert?
PEGGY	Only the Max Factor representative all the way from Winnipeg!
BILLY, 11	Wow!
PEGGY	He's been in Regina this week and normally wouldn't even bother stopping in Moose Jaw, but he knows there's a bit of magic afoot at Ruggles Rexall, so he's coming to see for himself. Ken! Let's go!
BILLY, 11	What's he coming to see, Mum?
PEGGY	Yours truly, young man, that's who. You may not know it, Billy, but your mum is the biggest-selling distributor of Max Factor in southern Saskatchewan. I don't mean to toot my own horn, but some say Peggy Ruggles has single-handedly brought beauty and glamour to the women of Moose Jaw.
BILLY, 11	Wow! What are you going to have for lunch, Mum?
PEGGY	What all the city career gals have, Billy. Chef's salad, garlic toast, and a Tab.
BILLY, 11	Wow!

KEN Ruggles enters. He's an attractive, albeit somewhat nondescript, man.

KEN And maybe a bit of Robert for dessert, Peg?

PEGGY Ken Ruggles, you hush! This is a purely professional luncheon date. Robert has no such interest in me, you know that.

KEN Yes Peggy, I know. Robert will be too busy winking at me to notice you.

PEGGY Well there you go, you can have Robert for dessert.

BILLY, 11 What does that mean, Mum?

PEGGY It means that… well, Billy… you see, Robert's… special. He's… from Winnipeg.

BILLY, 11 What does that mean? Dad?

KEN It means that some people from big cities are different, Billy.

BILLY, 11 How?

KEN Well, some people are… bohemians.

BILLY, 11 What's that?

KEN	Well Billy… artsy types. Like on CBC.
BILLY, 11	Like puppeteers?
KEN	I would imagine so, son.
BILLY, 11	I'm going to be a puppeteer!
PEGGY	What you're going to be is late for school if we don't get a move on. Now, I'm just going to take some pork chops out of the freezer, and when I get back you two better be ready to roll.

PEGGY exits.

BILLY, 11	Dad, I got a puppet book from the library that has plans for a marionette stage.
KEN	Oh Billy, you know I'm not very good with woodworking.
BILLY, 11	Yeah, but it's a professional stage, like real puppeteers use. It's plywood, Dad! And it shows what screws and nuts and hinges and stuff to use. It's big, but it folds up. And it fits in a car. Please. Please, Dad?
KEN	I'm sorry, son. I'm not one of those dads who knows how to make things, you know that. I'm a pharmacist, Billy, not a carpenter.

BILLY turns away and is silent, obviously disappointed. KEN moves toward him and places a hand on BILLY's shoulder.

It doesn't mean I don't know how to do other things.

BILLY, 11	Yeah, but none of it's stuff I like.
KEN	That's not true.
BILLY, 11	Yes it is. You don't know how to make puppets or stages or anything I like.
KEN	No, but I can make an appointment with Mr. Nadouwally.
BILLY, 11	So? What does he know, he's just a stupid travel agent.
KEN	Well, I think he probably knows lots of things, Billy.

BILLY, 11	Like what?
	KEN crouches down and turns BILLY so they're looking eye to eye.
KEN	I bet he knows how to reserve a seat on an airplane to Detroit, Michigan.
BILLY, 11	Yeah?
KEN	Yes sirree, I bet he does. Isn't that where the big puppetry festival is this summer?
BILLY, 11	Yeah.
KEN	And isn't that what you told your mother you wanted to do more than anything?
BILLY, 11	Yeah. But she said I couldn't go.
KEN	Billy, haven't you learned by now? You work your puppets, I'll manipulate your mother.
BILLY, 11	You're the best dad ever!
	BILLY hugs KEN.
KEN	Now remember, mum's the word.
	PEGGY enters.
PEGGY	All right, I've got the last box of Shake and Bake on the counter and the pork chops are thawing, so when we get home we'll have a nice nutritious dinner.... And what are you two jokers grinning about?
KEN	Nothing, dear. We were just saying how nice it will be for you to see Robert again.
	BILLY and KEN laugh, conspiratorially.
PEGGY	I see. Well, let me know when you two comedians are booked on the *Ed Sullivan Show* and I'll be sure to watch your act. For now, let's get this show on the road.
	PEGGY exits. KEN starts to follow when he is stopped by BILLY.
BILLY, 11	Dad?
KEN	Yes, son?

BILLY, 11	Are there bohemians in Detroit too?
KEN	Millions.
BILLY, 11	Wow!

They exit together.

Transition. The marionettes are hung back upstage, and the light dims somewhat on the marionette playing area as it re-establishes on BILLY standing on the bridge. SID appears by his side.

SID	I always thought your father to be a magnificent man, albeit with the characteristic flaw of comparing artists to sodomites.
BILLY	My dad was a great guy.
SID	Indeed. Precisely the kind of lineage that would cause one such morbid despair as to jump off a boat.
BILLY	Ship.
SID	What?
BILLY	It's a ship.
SID	You make me crazy, you know that, don't you? But you always have.
BILLY	I worshipped you.
SID	Exactly.

ৡ৶   ৶৶

THE SORCERER'S APPRENTICE

Transition to a flashback. Lights dim on the bridge and the handpuppet of SID is put away as BILLY brings two new marionettes into the playing area below him.

As lights restore on the marionette stage, we see BILLY, age twelve. This marionette version of him holds a dazzling, smaller marionette, strung onto a miniature control in puppet-BILLY's hand. The miniature puppet is of a scantily clad showgirl, dripping—some might say drowning—in sequins and an ostrich feather boa. Another boy marionette enters the scene. It is BENJI, also twelve years old. He is not an attractive boy; in fact, BENJI is a bespeckled geek who, while awkward in appearance and displaying a lack of poise, possesses the self-assurance of a know-it-all.

BENJI That's a nice puppet.

BILLY, 12 Thanks.

BENJI Where'd you get it?

BILLY, 12 I made it.

BENJI It's pretty good. I've only seen stripper puppets in books. Do her boobs rotate?

BILLY, 12 No. It's not a stripper; it's a showgirl.

BENJI Same thing.

BILLY, 12 No. Showgirls are dancers. And ladies. Strippers aren't as good.

BENJI Do her eyes move?

BILLY, 12 No. I don't know how to do that yet.

BENJI There's a workshop on moving eyes and mouths in half an hour.

BILLY, 12 I know; I'm going.

BENJI Me too.

BILLY, 12 Wanna sit together?

BENJI Okay. I'm Benji.

BILLY, 12 I'm Billy. Is this your first puppet festival too?

BENJI No, it's my second. I went to the last one in Pittsburgh. But it's way better here. What's your favourite part so far?

BILLY, 12 My favourite part hasn't happened yet. Sid Diamond is doing a marionette version of *The Taming of The Shrew*

on Thursday night. That's going to be my favourite part.

BENJI   He performed *Hamlet* at the Pittsburgh festival. It was boring. He talked too much.

BILLY, 12   It's Shakespeare.

BENJI   It was boring.

BILLY, 12	I'm gonna do Shakespeare someday.
BENJI	With a stripper?
BILLY, 12	It's not a stripper, it's a showgirl!
BENJI	We should go. The workshop is gonna start and I want to sit in the front row so I can ask all the questions.
BILLY, 12	Can you save me a seat? I'm kinda waiting for someone.
BENJI	Okay. But don't be late, 'k? Or I'll have to give your seat to someone I like better. And don't forget my name. It's Benji, and I'm gonna be the greatest puppeteer ever!

BENJI leaves.

BILLY, 12	Yeah, me too!

A marionette of SID Diamond, age fifty, enters.

Mr. Diamond?

SID, 50	Yes?
BILLY, 12	I wanted to show you my marionette.
SID, 50	Well, well, what have we here? That's very impressive, sir.
BILLY, 12	Oh, I'm not a sir. I'm Billy. Billy Ruggles.
SID, 50	Well, Mr. Ruggles, tell me, is there a puppet under all those feathers?
BILLY, 12	What? Yes. See?

BILLY jiggles the marionette.

I'm trying to put together a club act.

SID, 50	A club act, young man?
BILLY, 12	Yeah, you know, a variety show with trick marionettes. It might take a while though. But I already have the name: Billy Twinkle and His Stars in Miniature.
SID, 50	Billy Twinkle?
BILLY, 12	Yeah, that's me. Well, it will be.

SID, 50	Don't use that name. It's stupid.
BILLY, 12	I like it. It's sparkly.
SID, 50	It's Liberace, kid. And anywhere outside of Vegas, they'll kick your ass in the parking lot.
BILLY, 12	I like it.
SID, 50	It's your funeral. So, Mr. Twinkle, you want to be in showbiz then, not the theatre.
BILLY, 12	Both.
SID, 50	You can't be in both. They're different things.
BILLY, 12	Not in America.
SID, 50	You've figured this all out, haven't you?
BILLY, 12	I just need to finish school, get a green card, and build a bunch of puppets. Can I work for you?
SID, 50	I work alone.
BILLY, 12	Can I work with you?
SID, 50	Kid, enough. I don't take on apprentices.
BILLY, 12	I don't want to be an apprentice. I want to come stay with you and build puppets. You can show me your techniques. I'll bring a sleeping bag and sleep in the studio.
SID, 50	Well, you can't come stay with me. That's crazy. You're a kid. What would your parents say?
BILLY, 12	They said it's okay. I get three weeks at Easter break. I could come then. Christmas break is no good; I have a lot of shows booked already. It's just handpuppets, but I get fifty dollars a show. Woolworths on Friday nights and union Christmas parties at the Legion on Saturdays.
SID, 50	Why don't I just come stay with you? Sounds like you're getting all the work.
BILLY, 12	No, we don't have a band saw. And I know you do. You could show me.

SID, 50	What if I don't want to show you?
BILLY, 12	You have to.
SID, 50	Why?
BILLY, 12	Because I'm the next one. I'm gonna do it anyway, Mr. Diamond. And you could save me a lot of time if you just showed me how.
SID, 50	No one showed me how.
BILLY, 12	Yeah, but if they had, imagine where you'd be now.
SID, 50	You're something, Mr. Twinkle.
BILLY, 12	I'm not Billy Twinkle yet. My parents won't let me change it until I'm eighteen. I'm still just Billy Ruggles for now.
SID, 50	And how old are you, Mr. Ruggles?
BILLY, 12	Twelve. So, what about Easter? Can I come?
SID, 50	Have your parents come talk to me.
BILLY, 12	They're not here. They're at home in Moose Jaw.
SID, 50	Where the fuck is Moose Jaw?
BILLY, 12	It's in fucking Saskatchewan, Mr. Diamond.
SID, 50	And they let you come all the way to Detroit for a puppet festival by yourself?
BILLY, 12	They drove me to Regina. I flew on an airplane from there.
SID, 50	What kind of people send a twelve-year-old to a puppet festival by himself?
BILLY, 12	Mennonites. But we're townies; my dad owns the Rexall.
SID, 50	And your mother helped you sew the costume for your stripper?
BILLY, 12	It's not a stripper, Mr. Diamond. It's a showgirl. Like on Jackie Gleason and Ed Sullivan. I have to go. There's a workshop on moving eyes and mouths, and I don't want to miss it.

SID, 50	Waste of time, all that winking and blinking. I never animated my puppet faces.
BILLY, 12	I know, that's why I have to go to the workshop now. I figured that's something you won't be able to show me at Easter. But I'll sit with you at dinner, okay?
SID, 50	Well, a few of us old-timers are gonna sit together and visit.
BILLY, 12	That's okay. I'll just listen.
SID, 50	I'd like to see that, Mr. Ruggles.
BILLY, 12	Okay. See you later.

BILLY starts to leave.

And don't worry about Easter, I already know a lot. I've read all the puppet books in the library.

SID, 50	Well put the books aside and clear your mind of all that crap. I can't teach you anything if you learn all the wrong stuff from a bunch of books. Jesus Christ; Easter, huh?
BILLY, 12	Three weeks. You'll have to pick me up at the airport.
SID, 50	We'll discuss it at dinner. Well, go on, you'll miss your workshop.
BILLY, 12	I'm really glad I met you, Mr. Diamond. You're my favourite puppeteer.
SID, 50	Kid, you haven't even seen me perform yet.
BILLY, 12	That's okay. You've never seen me perform either.

BILLY leaves. SID watches him go and shakes his head as the lights fade on the scene.

Transition. Lights restore on BILLY and SID on the bridge.

THE SANDING OF TIME

BILLY	Huh.
SID	Huh? That's all you've got to say? Huh.
BILLY	I'd forgotten that.
SID	Lucky you. That was puppetry's blackest day. It haunts me still. Obviously.
BILLY	Look at me, I was really cute.
SID	That kid, as I recall, was a pain in the ass.
BILLY	Then why'd you let me come visit you that Easter, Sidney? And the next five summers after that?
SID	Do not flatter yourself, sir! You were nothing more than slave labour to me, paid with meals of beans and tuna-fish sandwiches and the occasional soupçon of theory thrown your way, which you gobbled up like a starving cur. Please, sir, do not romanticize those summer internments lest you deny me my joy in the memory of taking advantage of your zeal.
BILLY	Ah, sorry, Sid, but those summers were romantic.
SID	A pubescent boy obsessed with dolls is hardly a midsummer's dream, you ass. Have you forgotten the endless hours of sanding puppet parts that occupied those halcyon days of your youth?
BILLY	I fell in love with my craft because you put your puppets in my hands and made me touch them over and over again until I understood.
SID	Billy, you talk like a twelve-year-old schoolgirl. Really, sir, next you'll tell me you squat to pee! While you were sanding, all you felt were limbs, when in fact I had given you pieces of characters. Shylock! Iago! Titania and Prospero and Ophelia and Lear! I had waited each fall and winter and spring for you to bring me your juvenile *Dream* or awkward *Twelfth Night*. Yet with each passing summer, you brought me much ado about nothing. Strippers and juggling clowns and

cabaret singers. Tricks, Billy. Nothing but tricks. And there's no romance in that.

BILLY   Yes there was, Sid. It was sparkly. And it made the prairies seem like Hollywood.

Transition. SID is hung behind the leaning rail as lights cross-fade from the bridge to the stage below.

BETTY BOBBY AND BILLY

An upright piano is on stage. Seated there is Mrs. BETTY Bobby, a grinning older woman with a toothy overbite and a slight Scottish accent.

Fifteen-year-old BILLY stands beside her at the piano. He has obviously grown, and is that awkward and dangerously appealing mixture of boy and man.

As the light reveals them, we hear BETTY Bobby's enthusiastic piano accompaniment as BILLY sings. It is the end of some sort of folk/art song.

BILLY   "…and the gypsy's song was heard all around the world."

BETTY   That was fine, Billy, just fine. But remember, hold onto your vowels, dear. Keep them open as long as you can. It's "wooooooooorld," not "worrrrrrrrrld." We don't want to sound American, now do we?

BILLY, 15   Yes. That's where I'm going to work.

BETTY   Oh, so we've given up on Winnipeg, have we?

BILLY, 15   Um, no. But Winnipeg's just a stepping stone. I'm going to America, Mrs. Bobby. That's where showbiz is.

BETTY   I see. Well, before we send you out into the world, young man, humour me, Billy, and sing it like a Canadian. "Wooooooooorld."

BILLY, 15   Wooooooooorld.

BETTY   Better, but don't forget that consonant at the end. Without the "d" you're just in a "whirl," not the world.

It's like shutting a door, and we want to keep the flies out of your throat, don't we, Mr. Ruggles? Once more.

BILLY, 15   Wooooooooorld.

BETTY   Ladies and gentlemen, I present to you, a Canadian! Thank you, Billy. Shall we sing through it one more time from the beginning?

BILLY, 15   Could we sing something else instead, Mrs. Bobby?

BETTY   Of course. What do you suggest? "'Twas A Maiden By The Winding Road"?

BILLY, 15   No thanks.

BETTY   "Grant Me Succour, O Lamb of Love"?

BILLY, 15   Mrs. Bobby, could we sing this instead?

BILLY points to some sheet music on the piano, presumably behind the previous song.

BETTY   Oh, I see you've brought in some sheet music of your own! Very good, Billy.

> *She leans forward and looks at the music, reading its title aloud.*

Good Lord, what's this then? "Highfalutin' Lady From the Wrong Side of Town." Hmmm. I'm not familiar with this one, Billy. I don't believe it's in the Royal Conservatory syllabus.

BILLY, 15   It's jazz, Mrs. Bobby.

BETTY   Then it's definitely not in the syllabus.

BILLY, 15   My dad has a record of Delia Rivers singing it. It's really good, but I don't want to use the record. I want to sing it myself.

BETTY   Oh. You want to sing "Highfalutin' Lady…"

BILLY, 15   "…From the Wrong Side of Town."

BETTY   I see.

BILLY, 15   Can you help me with it?

BETTY   Hmmm. You're sure you wouldn't rather sing "Grant Me Succour, O Lamb of Love"?

BILLY, 15   Yup.

BETTY   Billy.

BILLY, 15   Sorry. I mean, yes, Mrs. Bobby, I'm sure.

BETTY   You do know, Billy, this song is for a woman to sing.

BILLY, 15   Yes.

BETTY   A certain kind of woman, Billy.

BILLY, 15   From the wrong side of town.

BETTY   Indeed.

BILLY, 15   And she's down in the dumps because she fell for a swell on the right side of town, and even with her gowns and feathers, fancy French perfume can't hide the fact that she's garbage. So he broke her heart and left her in the gutter. That's why she's singing this song.

BETTY   I see you've analyzed the tune, dear.

BILLY, 15   I already know the words.

BETTY	I have no doubt you do, Billy. But, you see, dear, this isn't the sort of song a young man of fifteen might sing in Moose Jaw. Why, I daresay it would be a tad controversial for the Kiwanis Music Festival, even in the looser category of Musical Theatre.
BILLY, 15	Oh, I'd never sing it there, Mrs. Bobby.
BETTY	Good to hear, dear.
BILLY, 15	I'm going to sing it at the Wagonwheel Lounge.
BETTY	The Wagonwheel?
BILLY, 15	Yeah. I mean, yes. The motel out on the Trans-Canada Highway. They've booked Stars in Miniature every Monday and Wednesday night for a month.
BETTY	Oh, Billy! Your wee puppets! Oh, you had me going there for a minute, dear. Oh! I thought you wanted to… well, you know… frock up.
BILLY, 15	Mrs. Bobby?
BETTY	Never mind, Billy. So, this is a song for a lady marionette!
BILLY, 15	I call her Randi Rivers. It's kind of like Delia Rivers, except she ain't no lady. I can say ain't 'cause it's jazz.
BETTY	I see.

BILLY sits beside her on the piano bench.

BILLY, 15	So, can you help me with it, Mrs. Bobby?
BETTY	But you already know it, Billy.
BILLY, 15	Yes, but I sound like me.
BETTY	Who else would you sound like, dear?
BILLY, 15	I want to sing like Delia Rivers.
BETTY	Billy… Delia Rivers was a woman, dear. And when she sang that song, she understood what it meant because she had lived through… well, certain things.
BILLY, 15	Men, right?
BETTY	Yes. Men. Do you understand me, Billy?

BILLY, 15	Kind of.
BETTY	Yes, I suspect you do.
BILLY, 15	It's a really nice puppet, Mrs. Bobby.
BETTY	I have no doubt of that, Billy.
BILLY, 15	So you'll help me?
BETTY	Well dear, this is a bit out of my league. Why, it's all jazzy and swingy, and Betty Bobby hasn't swung in years!

BILLY sighs, defeated. They are silent for a moment.

When's your first engagement at the Wagonwheel Lounge?

BILLY, 15	Three weeks.
BETTY	Three weeks?! Billy, what were you thinking? You should have brought this in three months ago, dear! And here we've been wasting all our time singing bloody folk songs! All right, let's get to work.
BILLY, 15	Oh thank you, Mrs. Bobby!
BETTY	Call me Betty.
BILLY, 15	Really?
BETTY	It's jazz, Billy. I don't think they call women "Mrs." in that world. And I have a feeling this is a whole new world for both of us.
BILLY, 15	Don't you mean wooooooooorld, Betty?
BETTY	I most certainly do not! Jazz is American, Billy. So let's not be hanging onto those vowels, Miss Randi Rivers!

BETTY attacks the piano, playing a ham-fisted intro to "Highfalutin' Lady From the Wrong Side of Town." BILLY sings, initially sounding like himself, but as the lights fade, his voice becomes smokier, more nuanced, and while perhaps not "realistic," mimics the qualities of a female jazz singer.

"HIGHFALUTIN' LADY FROM THE WRONG SIDE OF TOWN"
Music and Lyrics by John Alcorn

BILLY, 15 My furs are fancy, but worn and dusty
'Cause I wear them all year roun'
I'm just a highfalutin' lady
From the wrong side of town.

BETTY Let's move up a tone, dear.

BILLY, 15 My Daddy told me to hide his pistol
Underneath my velvet gown.
Yes, I'm a highfalutin' lady
From the wrong side of town.

> *The marionettes of BETTY Bobby and BILLY are removed. All the while, the song continues in dim light, and when it restores, we see BILLY standing atop the piano in a spotlight. He is the same age as in the previous scene, but now dressed in tight toreador pants and rumba sleeves. This marionette BILLY is manipulating a smaller marionette of Randi Rivers, a plump black woman dressed in a sparkling gown and feather boa with an orchid in her hair.*

I'm his woman ev'ry Saturday night, makin' lazy love
When lights are low, there's nothing that he lacks.
But ev'ry Sunday morn, he drives his Cadillac home
To the right side of the tracks.
Right to the bottom of ev'ry bottle,
Let me drink my liquor down,
'Cause when that Cadillac horn comes a-tootin',
And my man's pistol starts a-shootin'
I've got to be his highfalutin' lady
From the wrong side of town.

> *As the spotlight fades, the number comes to an end. A middle-aged man in a suit and glasses approaches BILLY.*

OUT OF THE SUPPLY CLOSET

THE MAN	That was quite the act. Real different.
BILLY, 15	I don't think they liked it.
THE MAN	Oh, they were just a bit annoyed the hockey game got turned down. They're fine now. So, what'dya call that?
BILLY, 15	It's called Stars in Miniature.
THE MAN	Yeah, I got that part. But the thing you do with those dolls…
BILLY, 15	Marionettes. They're not dolls.
THE MAN	Sorry, marionettes. That's a fancy word.
BILLY, 15	It's French.
THE MAN	I see. So, that thing you do with them… must be hard.
BILLY, 15	The puppets are the easy part. Well, if you build them right and practise a lot. It's the audience that's hard.
THE MAN	You must work up quite the sweat.
BILLY, 15	Uh huh. These sleeves are hot. And the pants are pretty tight.
THE MAN	So I noticed. Where would you find a getup like that?
BILLY, 15	The skating club. They were doing Fiesta on Ice, but Kyle Nazinsky got teased too much and dropped out. He's doing hockey now instead. So they sold me the costume for five dollars.
THE MAN	Well, it suits you.
BILLY, 15	You think so?
THE MAN	Sure. Real Las Vegas-looking.
BILLY, 15	Have you been to Las Vegas?
THE MAN	Twice.
BILLY, 15	Wow. What's it like?
THE MAN	Well, it's different. Real sexy-like.
BILLY, 15	Wow.

THE MAN   You like sexy, don't you?

BILLY, 15   Um, sure.

THE MAN   I could tell.

BILLY, 15   Yeah?

THE MAN	Sure. That lady there, she's pretty darn sexy, don't you think?
	He indicates the marionette in BILLY's hand.
BILLY, 15	Her name is Randi Rivers. She's a floozy, but it's not her fault. A man did her wrong.
THE MAN	I see. Buy you a drink?
BILLY, 15	No. Thanks. I can't.
THE MAN	I thought you'd be thirsty after that show.
BILLY, 15	I am, but I gotta go. Home.
THE MAN	Hmmm. School in the morning, huh?
BILLY, 15	Yeah. I mean, yes. Well, no.
THE MAN	How old are you?
BILLY, 15	Old enough. To drink, I mean. I drink all the time.
THE MAN	I see. So you must be, what? Eighteen or nineteen?
BILLY, 15	Okay.
THE MAN	Seventeen? Sixteen?
BILLY, 15	Sure.
THE MAN	Fifteen?
	BILLY is silent.
	Fifteen. Well, well, well.
BILLY, 15	Please don't tell.
THE MAN	I wasn't gonna, but don't they already know?
BILLY, 15	They didn't ask. And they only pay me ten bucks a night, so I don't think they care.
THE MAN	Well, how about that drink then?
BILLY, 15	I can't.
THE MAN	I said I wouldn't tell.
BILLY, 15	I can't. It's unprofessional to mingle with the public after a performance. In my costume, I mean.

THE MAN	Oh, sure. Why don't we get you out of that costume then. I've never seen a real professional dressing room before.
BILLY, 15	Neither have I. I change in the supply closet in the kitchen.
THE MAN	Hardly seems right, a big star like you changing in the kitchen.
BILLY, 15	I'm not a big star.
THE MAN	You will be.
BILLY, 15	You think so?
THE MAN	I know so. You got a real unique talent there and you're as pretty as anything I've seen in Las Vegas.
BILLY, 15	Boys can't be pretty.
THE MAN	Some boys are. You are, Billy. You're a real pretty boy.
BILLY, 15	Um, thanks.
THE MAN	Look, I'm just passing through on business, so I've got a room here at the Wagonwheel all to myself. What say we get you out of that closet and change you in my room?
BILLY, 15	I… I dunno…
THE MAN	You could have a shower too. I got a stack of clean white towels.
BILLY, 15	I gotta call my dad. He picks me up.
THE MAN	It won't take long. Whatta you say?
BILLY, 15	Okay.
THE MAN	Okay.

The light snaps abruptly to the playing area above to BILLY and SID.

| SID | Okay, okay, okay! That's enough of that! |
| BILLY | Yeah, I could feel your sphincter getting tight. My hand's practically numb. |

SID	What are you implying, sir?
BILLY	Come on, Sid. Straight men always clench their assholes whenever things start getting a bit gay.
SID	Enough! You're not funny, Billy. Why, that was verging on illegal.
BILLY	I'm not the one who built the puppets, Sid. Why did you make me remember him anyway?

BILLY hangs the marionettes backstage.

SID	Gee, I don't know, Billy. Call me crazy, but I assumed being raped was a pivotal moment in your life!
BILLY	I wasn't raped. I wanted to. I let him.
SID	He took advantage of you!
BILLY	We took advantage of each other. Sound familiar, Sid?
SID	I never once laid a hand on you!
BILLY	No, that might have shown some affection.
SID	Billy, I'm not that way!
BILLY	I know, Sid. I know. You can relax. You're not my type anyway.
SID	Really? Why not?
BILLY	Piss off, Sid.
SID	Well, you must admit, I am a handsome fellow.
BILLY	Sid…
SID	I mean, I could hardly blame you for being attracted to me.
BILLY	Sid…
SID	Strong jaw, magnificent nose, broad shoulders…
BILLY	Bunny ears…
SID	Fuck you. Admit it, Billy, you find me attractive.
BILLY	No, I don't.
SID	Then pray tell, sir, why is your hand so sweaty?

In frustration, BILLY buries his face in his arm resting on the leaning rail.

BILLY   I need a drink.

SID   Say, are you still doing that drunken society dame number? Hilarious! I loved that routine.

BILLY   You hated that routine.

SID   Did not!

BILLY   Did so!

SID   Let's see it again.

BILLY   No.

SID   Hit it, boys!

Without warning, the lavish intro to the Billy Twinkle show theme music begins. The Mylar backdrop for BILLY's act is drawn closed in front of the marionette stage and lighting becomes showbiz theatrical again. SID is hung behind the leaning rail, and BILLY rushes down the stairs and puts on his tuxedo jacket.

A marionette-scale table is set CS. It is circular and covered with a damask tablecloth. Sitting on the table is a full wineglass with a straw. The glass is fixed to a rig, which, when operated by a foot peddle, causes the liquid to "disappear" underneath.

BILLY takes the marionette of BIDDY Bantam Brewster from under the stairs. She is a strongly caricatured society dame wearing an outrageous chartreuse green velvet gown festooned with chiffon rosettes. As the music ends, BILLY sweeps BIDDY onto the main playing area of the deck. She plays directly to the audience.

BIDDY BANTAM BREWSTER

BIDDY Hello! Hello! Hello! And welcome to this, another afternoon recital of "Wine, Woman, and Song." I, your hostess, Biddy Bantam Brewster, am of course the woman who will serenade you with song, while you, dear gathered friends and lovers of music, enjoy the complimentary wine, provided this afternoon by the lovely people at Dirtroad Estates Winery and Feedlot, conveniently located near the civic dump off Highway 71.

BIDDY "drinks."

Oh my, that's quite nice! A good week, that. A subtle hint of pork mixed with the stronger notes of the grape. I find the use of a straw is so much more genteel, don't you think? And it prevents my lipstick from escaping onto the glass.

She takes another long sip.

Some of you may recall our previous "Wine, Woman, and Song" concert, when I performed an aria from Giancarlo Sacchetto del Vento's controversial opera *La Padrona del Diavolo,* or, *The Devil's Mistress,* in which I sang the titular role of Sister Serafina, a wayward nun who, at the conclusion of Act One, sings the beautiful and haunting "O Dio, Il mio pannello esterno è su fuoco," which, roughly translated, means "Oh God, my skirt is on fire." The audience was so visibly moved by my performance that many of you personally thanked me for not singing Acts Two and Three. Come on you bloody grape, give Mummy what she wants...

She drinks again and burps.

Why, after my last "Wine, Woman, and Song," I received comments such as "It chilled me to the bone," and "Thank you for the wine, I really needed it," and, of course, my favourite, "Truly a once-in-a-lifetime experience. I hope."

BIDDY has another sip.

But these sorts of comments have not been uncommon in my career. Why, I remember my one and only lesson with the great German singing teacher, Professor Emil Pelznüsse of the famous Berlin Korrespondenzkonservatorium der Mechaniker und der Kunst. I had been exploring my *kunst* privately ever since I was a girl, but felt it was time to take my *kunst* abroad and have a professional really stretch me. I arrived demanding, "Take me to your Lieder!" and when I sang for him, Professor Pelznüsse announced that I had lubricated his *schadenfreude* to the point of no return. For which I thanked him, while gently reminding him that I was a married woman. No, the purpose of our Teutonic tryst that memorable afternoon was to service my throat, for I simply had to sing in the worst possible way. Showing me to the door, the professor assured me that indeed I had.

What a dear, dear man.

> *She drinks again.*

It was on that fateful day I decided to share my gift with any and all who loved music. And even those of you who don't. So I devised my plan to entice you into my salon, sedate you with wine, and seduce you with song. And by your appreciative half-lidded gaze I can tell you're quite pleased to be here. Or anywhere, for that matter.

> *She drinks again.*

And I couldn't be happier to see you! Hello! Hello! Hello!

> *BIDDY leers at the audience.*

Who are you people? What the hell are you doing in my house?

> *The musical accompaniment begins.*

Oh yes, of course. You're here for the wine! The woman! And the song!

> *BIDDY sings. This is a full-on number, beginning simply and "classically" enough with gypsy violin accompaniment, but one that veers quickly into a drunken comedy number.*

"RAISINETTE"

Music and Lyrics by John Alcorn

BIDDY
Long, long ago in a land far away
Lived a gypsy, a lady gypsy.
Succulent, fulsome, the loveliest grape
On the vine.
Burning with youth and ablaze with desire
Was this gypsy, this pretty gypsy.
Ne'er was the candle that burn'd half so bright
As her flame.
Sure that a brave gypsy king she would wed
Was this gypsy, this bitsy gypsy.
Head full of fancy, each callow young swain
She'd decline.
Tossing her curls as she danced the flamenco
This gypsy, this frisky gypsy.
Flashing her eyes as the vagabond boys
Called her name.

Raisinette
How she'd pirouette
To the throbbing sound
Of drum or castanet.
Raisinette
What a fate she met,
Like some floozy from
A dime-store novelette
Men forget
Girls like Raisinette
When they change their tunes
From solo to duet.
Still, she dances on through the night
Dreaming of her lover's delight,
The day he marries
Raisinette.

> *There is a brief dance break, ending with a cancan,*
> *at which point BIDDY picks up her skirt and reveals*
> *a sea of white ruffles, her lace bloomers, and red*
> *stockings.*

Drunken with moonlight, he plucked her and
Plundered her hist'ry, pathetic gypsy,
Miserable, slowly she's drowning in cheap
Spanish wine.
Staggering now, where she once used to dance,
Is it whiskey? Poor, tipsy gypsy.
Gone is her glory, her beauty, her youth,
And her fame.

Raisinette,
Cast away coquette
Withered on the vine,
A sodden, old soubrette,
Raisinette,
Though her eyes are wet,
Can't remember what
She's drinking to forget.
With regret
Lives our Raisinette,
For he graped her thrice
And tossed her vinaigrette.

Still, she dances on through the night
Dreaming of her lover's delight,
The day he marries
Raisinette

Raisinette

Raisinette

Raisinette!

> *At the conclusion of BIDDY's act, BILLY strikes the
> marionette and table under the stairs and removes
> his jacket. A play out of BIDDY's song underscores
> this action and transition. BILLY climbs the stairs,
> opens the Mylar curtain, and brings a marionette on
> stage. Light settles there to reveal BENJI, age twenty-
> five. This is no longer the awkward geek we met at
> age twelve, although BENJI is no more attractive
> and still freckled and bespeckled. He has embraced
> the look of a 1980s neo-Romantic artist/club kid and*

*wears skin-tight black pants, leg warmers, velvet
Peter Pan boots, and a ruffled pirate shirt. His hair is
a wild shock of orange disarray.*

SMOKE GETS IN YOUR ASS

BENJI, 25   Billy! Billy Twinkle! Where are you, man? Billy!

*BILLY, age twenty-five, appears dressed in overalls,
a red gingham shirt, and a cowboy hat.*

BILLY, 25   I'm here. Hello?

BENJI, 25   Billy, it's me. Benji.

BILLY, 25   Benji, wow! Hi. I was so excited when I heard you were coming to this festival.

BENJI, 25   I wasn't, man. What was I thinking, coming to a puppet festival again? But now I know why the forces drew me here. It was to see your show, Billy.

BILLY, 25   Get out, you saw Stars in Miniature this afternoon?

BENJI, 25   Billy, it was so cool. You are amazing, man. When that society dame got drunk I thought I was going to piss myself. Fucking brilliant.

BILLY, 25   It's a standard old routine, Benji.

BENJI, 25   In the hands of a twisted modernist. What are you anyway? Psychic? Alien? Jesus Christ returned to heal puppetry's evil ways? You rock this scene, Billy!

BILLY, 25   I'm glad you liked it.

BENJI, 25   No! I did not like it, man. It slapped me across the face. It slapped me in the ass. It slapped my dead heart into beating again. It's pure, Billy. You're like an angel from the frozen north, untouched by all the hot shit that's going around.

BILLY, 25   Benji, stop blowing smoke up my ass, okay?

BENJI, 25   I'm not, Billy. I'm worshipping you, man. Take the love.

BILLY, 25	Since when have you liked what I do? You hate marionettes.
BENJI, 25	No! I hate the marionettes of the past that enslaved us in the polite European post-industrial mechanics of form, man. But you've opened my eyes, Billy, and now I see. You're a visionary, man, leading us into the light of a brave neo day.
BILLY, 25	No I'm not. Hey Benji, guess what? It was just a puppet show. That's all. A marionette variety show.
BENJI, 25	You tease me, God of Puppetry. While the rest of us are breaking our balls busting the form wide open, you found the key. The secret. You knew to leave well enough alone. Do it the old way, like it's always been done. Don't change a thing. But your act changed my life, Billy, because I've already seen it before. Oh man, it's so simple. It's so beautiful. Now I know, there is no new in art. You, Billy Twinkle, are a true celestial being. May I kiss your feet?
BILLY, 25	Benj, stop it.
BENJI, 25	Yeah, I guess I should. I got my show tonight and our tech is fucked.
BILLY, 25	I can't wait to see it, Benji. This is the one with all the video, right?
BENJI, 25	Fifty screens filled with static representing our disconnected land.
BILLY, 25	Wow. How many puppets?
BENJI, 25	None. I'm the puppet, you know?
BILLY, 25	Oh. Well, I can't wait to see it.
BENJI, 25	It's a piece of shit, Billy. You'll hate it.
BILLY, 25	The press love it. They're calling you the greatest puppeteer in the world.
BENJI, 25	The press sucked my cock and spit my essence all over their cheap, filthy newsprint. Be glad you're not famous, man. Stay pure, little cowboy.

	BENJI exits.
SID, 63	*(offstage)* Pssst. Pssst!
BILLY, 25	Hello?
SID, 63	*(offstage)* Billy! Pssst!
	SID, age sixty-three, enters.

ᔓ   ᔕ

THE TAMING OF THE MOO

SID, 63	Billy, thank God! Grant me shelter, sir, for I've been sighted by that obsequious hobbyist, Doreen Gray. If she corners me with her mitten puppets I'll never escape.
BILLY, 25	Sid!
	SID eyes BILLY's attire.
SID, 63	Billy, is there a hoedown I've not been apprised of?
BILLY, 25	It's a costume. I was just rehearsing.
SID, 63	Oh? Something new?
BILLY, 25	Yeah, you know… just goofing around.
SID, 63	I see. And when might this new folly of yours be presented to your peers and public?
BILLY, 25	Tomorrow.
SID, 63	My, two performances in one festival. Very ambitious, Billy. I caught your… what do you call your little variety show again?
BILLY, 25	Stars in Miniature.
SID, 63	Yes, of course. I caught your Stars in Miniature performance this afternoon.
BILLY, 25	Oh.
	There's an awkward silence between them.
SID, 63	It was good.

BILLY, 25	Thanks.
SID, 63	For that sort of thing. The drunken diva…
BILLY, 25	Biddy Bantam Brewster.
SID, 63	Yes, Madam Brewster.

Awkward silence.

It was good.

BILLY, 25	Thanks.
SID, 63	Yes. Good.
BILLY, 25	But?
SID, 63	No buts. No.

Awkward silence again.

Although, I wonder how many times we have to see a puppeteer doing a drag act with a comic opera singer. There's nothing new there, Billy.

BILLY, 25	How many times do we have to see Shakespeare, Sid? Nothing new there either, but people still do it.
SID, 63	Touché! Even if you disregard that the magic lies in the personal interpretation of those timeless words. But I'm interrupting your rehearsal, which no doubt you need.

SID turns and starts to leave.

BILLY, 25	Hey Sid… do you wanna watch? I'd really like your opinion.
SID, 63	I'm flattered, Billy. Although, inane cabaret turns have never been my forte; no, that is more your dominion. I really don't see what help I could be.
BILLY, 25	It's Shakespeare.
SID, 63	You're doing a Shakespeare?
BILLY, 25	Do you mind?
SID, 63	Mind? Billy, I have waited years to hear you say this. At times, I thought I never would. There were moments

when I despaired over having wasted my time on you. What took you so long to submit to my influence, to hear the Bard's whispers, to see the light? But now, at last!

He hugs BILLY enthusiastically.

"Bless thee, Bottom, bless thee! Thou art translated."

True, by the time I was twenty-five, I'd already done four substantial productions, but better late than never. All right, let's see what you've got. Show me your stuff, kid.

BILLY runs offstage. Music begins. The red velvet curtain is closed and the lighting shifts to a more theatrical pool CS.

BILLY reappears, a duplicate of the BILLY at age twenty-five marionette, and he has in his hands two marionettes. They are somewhat larger than the small puppets used in the scenes of BILLY at ages twelve and fifteen.

Petruchio, renamed PETROOSTER for this version, has the head of a rooster and a humanesque body. PETROOSTER is in brightly coloured Elizabethan garb, with his muscular legs encased in tights and a very noticeable cod piece. Kate, renamed for this interpretation as COWTRINA is, indeed, a cow, anthropomorphized to the point of standing on two legs in cloven high-heel hooves. A pink udder juts out from her faux-Elizabethan gown.

PETROOSTER   "Good morrow, Kate, for that's your name, I hear."

COWTRINA   "Well have you heard, but something hard of hearing; They call me Cowtrina that do talk of me."

PETROOSTER   "You lie, in faith, for you are call'd plain Kate, And bonny Kate, and sometimes Kate the curst; But Kate, the prettiest Kate in Christendom, Kate of Kate Hall, my super-dainty Kate, For dainties all are Kates, and therefore, Kate, Take this of me, Kate of my consolation;

Having thy mildness prais'd in every town,
Thy virtues spoke of, and thy beauty sounded,
Yet not so deeply as to thee belongs,
Myself am mov'd to woo thee for my wife."

COWTRINA "Moved! In good time: let him that mov'd you hither
Remove you hence. I knew you at the first
You were a movable."

PETROOSTER "Why, what's a movable?"

COWTRINA "A join'd stool."

PETROOSTER "Thou hast hit it: come, sit on me."

COWTRINA "Asses are made to bear, and so are you."

PETROOSTER "Women are made to bear, and so are you."

SID interrupts the show.

SID, 63 And I can bear no more! Billy, please. Stop. I beg of you.

The performance stops, and the marionettes of PETROOSTER and COWTRINA droop lifelessly in BILLY's hands.

BILLY, 25 What's wrong, Sid?

SID, 63 I have a question, sir.

BILLY, 25 Okay.

SID, 63 Tell me, was it your intention to have the Bard roll over in his grave so you could fuck him up the ass?

BILLY, 25 What are you talking about?

SID, 63 I'm talking about the bullshit you were just doing with that pig and chicken.

BILLY, 25 It's not a pig, Sid, it's a cow. It's *The Taming of the Moo.*

SID, 63 Oh Christ!

BILLY, 25 The text was there. I was word perfect and you know it.

SID, 63 You took the text to the barnyard and buried it in pig shit!

BILLY, 25	Cow shit!
SID, 63	Whatever!
BILLY, 25	Admit it, Sid. You didn't like it because it had a cow and a rooster, that's all. Why do you hate animal puppets so much, Sid? It's like a sickness with you.
SID, 63	Your puppets are supposed to be reinventions of self. To edify, to exalt, and yes, to mock and even condemn our graceless state. But is this how you want to be seen? As livestock?
BILLY, 25	Who says they're reinventions of me or you, Sid? They're characters, that's all.
SID, 63	And if that's all you invest in them, sir, cleverness and parody, well, then that's all the audience will take away. Unless of course the point is not the text or the characters at all, Billy. Yes, of course, there's no need for more of you in the words or the characters because that would mean we'd stop looking at you.
BILLY, 25	It's called open manipulation, Sid.
SID, 63	You're visible simply for the sake of being seen, pretty boy! Your focus is nowhere near the puppets at all; standing above them, mugging and posturing like a powdered vaudevillian playing God. We don't need you to be God. We don't want you to be God. There's already a God on stage, and it's not you. It's the goddamn puppet!
BILLY, 25	You tell me I'm not God, but I'm supposed to manipulate Him. Which is more arrogant, Sid?
SID, 63	Arrogance is to have the ability and not use it. To create something that breathes, that truly lives inside your audience long after the puppet stops twitching.
BILLY, 25	They're not alive, Sid. They're puppets. And the audience leaves. They go home, without you. Jiggle jiggle, ha ha, end of story, end of play, exeunt all.
SID, 63	Is that all you retained from Shakespeare, Billy? Exeunt all?

BILLY, 25	At least I know what it means, Sid. Get off the stage.
	SID is silent and still for a moment, then turns and exits.

LESLIE KAYE SERA SERA

BILLY watches SID leave.

BILLY, 25	You're not the only one who can do Shakespeare, Sid. I'm the new God of puppetry!
	LESLIE Kaye enters. He is a short, elderly man; immaculately groomed, with a sweep of white hair and a pencil-thin moustache. He speaks softly, with a slight Southern accent.
LESLIE	I'm sorry to interrupt. Is this a bad time?
BILLY, 25	Oh God, how embarrassing.
LESLIE	Allow me to introduce myself. Leslie Kaye.
BILLY, 25	I know. I love your work. I'm sorry, hi, I'm Billy.
LESLIE	I found your Stars in Miniature to be the most delightful new interpretation of the classic marionette variety show.
BILLY, 25	Really?
LESLIE	Indeed, sir. And from the little bit I was just able to spy, I think *The Taming of the Moo* verges on genius, sir!
BILLY, 25	Really? Some people think I've gone too far, Mr. Kaye.
LESLIE	On the contrary, Billy, you've not gone far enough. Trust your instincts. They will lead you down the most interesting paths.
BILLY, 25	Or a dead end.
LESLIE	That's the point of youth. You still have time to turn around and retrace your steps. I no longer have the benefit of youth myself, Billy, and I simply cannot handle all my bookings for nightclubs and cruise ships. And frankly, I'm not certain that audiences want to see

	an old dear like myself wiggling his dollies in slow motion.
BILLY, 25	You look great, Mr. Kaye.
LESLIE	You're a polite boy, Billy. Thank your mother for me. No, while I still would like to accept engagements, I feel it's time to send a younger person out on the road. And when I saw your performance this afternoon I realized I had found him.
BILLY, 25	Are you offering me a job, Mr. Kaye?
LESLIE	No. I'm offering you a career, Billy. It can be a wonderful life if you let it. Nightclubs are dying off, but the cruise-ship industry is about to explode, so it's a sea of possibilities. Have you ever cruised, Billy?
BILLY, 25	Um, no.
LESLIE	Something tells me you'll take to it like a fish to water. What do you say? Would you be interested in relocating to California and working with me?
BILLY, 25	I'd love to, Mr. Kaye, but I haven't had any luck working in the States. All you have to say at Immigration is "I'm a puppeteer" and suddenly you're in a room with a finger up your ass.
LESLIE	How delightful. Remind me to travel more often. Don't you worry, Billy. I'll arrange your visa, and if things work out, perhaps in time it'll be a green card.
BILLY, 25	Wow, that would be... a dream come true, Mr. Kaye.
LESLIE	Now sir, I insist you call me Leslie. We're about to be colleagues, Billy.
BILLY, 25	Thank you, Leslie. I won't let you down.
LESLIE	Of course not, why on earth would you?

Music in as light cross-fades up to the bridge where BILLY is looking down at the younger marionette of himself. SID handpuppet pops up.

Paved with Gold

SID	I can't believe you ran off with that preening poodle Leslie Kaye! You broke my heart, Billy.
BILLY	Well how was I to know? I didn't hear from you for the next twenty years!
SID	Believe me, sir, if I had my way, I wouldn't be here now!
BILLY	So why are you here now? Oh yes, I remember. To fix your sad, dead, broken heart!
SID	No, to help you break yours.
BILLY	What kind of bullshit is that, Sid?

> *BILLY leaves the bridge and walks down the SR stairs. Obviously, SID follows him.*

	Why would I want to break my own heart?
SID	So you can feel something again.
BILLY	I feel!
SID	No you don't.
BILLY	I was standing on the edge of a boat trying to kill myself, Sidney!
SID	Feeling nothing! Typical, you give up just when it's getting good.
BILLY	It never gets good for me, Sid!
SID	Boo hoo! Lazy! Whiner! Quitter!
BILLY	All I've ever done is work!
SID	In your comfort zone! Sloth! Coward! Dilettante!
BILLY	Shut up!
SID	Blamer! Weakling! Sissy!

> *BILLY throws SID, and by extension himself, to the floor and pins him there, hovering over him menacingly.*

BILLY	Shut the fuck up, old man.

SID   What are you going to do, Billy… kill me?

BILLY releases SID and sits up.

BILLY   My whole life…. Ever since I was a kid, your voice in my head. It doesn't matter if you're alive or dead because there you are, the great Sid Diamond, telling me to be better. Well guess what? I'm not. I can't be. I can't be you.

And that's all I ever wanted to be.

There is silence between them. BILLY sits facing upstage, his focus down. The handpuppet SID sits on BILLY's shoulder facing out, his little legs dangling.

SID   When I started working, there were a handful of us trying to make a go of it professionally. They were my competition, but we had a bond in this crazy notion that we could keep ourselves fed doing puppet shows. Not that any of us did the same show, but we made marionettes into something special. Not the jerky flash and dazzle of the music-hall turns; oh no, we were the cocky new kids determined to show that puppets were serious business.

It was hard going. I drove endless dirt roads just to take Shakespeare in miniature to people who had never seen a marionette or heard such words before. *Othello* in the deep South. Farmers witnessing their first *Midsummer Night's Dream*. *The Merchant of Venice* in churches and factory canteens, *The Tempest* in schools along the Atlantic and Pacific, *Twelfth Night* for months on end, coast to coast and back again. And always, always *Hamlet* and *The Taming of the Shrew*, for in those uncertain times we needed to wonder at life and laugh, too. Me and my puppets on those endless dirt roads.

It was glorious.

The golden age of American puppetry. And not one of us knew it was the golden age. By the time our heyday was deemed golden, we were dead, dying, or on TV. Television killed the great American puppet renaissance. And my little Globe was not welcome in that brave new world. End of the road.

And at the end of my road, Billy, there you were. Twelve years old; so rosy, so hungry and pious, and an absolute outrage. You moved me. And I stood running on the spot long after I could move, just waiting to pass the torch to you. But that little boy disappeared from my life for twenty years. Why Billy? Why did you drift away just when I needed that golden boy to run ahead? I paved the road for you.

> *SID strokes BILLY's hair, then "stands" above him. That is, BILLY's arm extends straight up with SID looking down.*

Come on.

> *BILLY follows SID up the stairs to the bridge. Music and lighting cover the transition, during which the handpuppet of SID is hung on the back of the leaning rail and BILLY places two marionettes on the playing area.*

> *We see SID, now age eighty-three. He is noticeably older, and his posture quite crooked from age. He is holding a smaller marionette of Juliet. She is one of his puppets; graceful, elegant, detailed but not fussy. And because she is a marionette of a lovesick teenage girl in the hands of an elderly man, Juliet is perhaps even more delicate.*

> *BILLY enters, now age forty-five. He's dressed in a very elaborate midnight blue tuxedo, the jacket of which is beaded in a silver-and-gold star motif. BILLY has gotten very fat, and even the cinched cummerbund around his waist cannot hide his girth. He holds a miniature marionette of BIDDY Bantam Brewster.*

BILLY, 45   Sid?

> *SID looks up from his marionette and sees BILLY.*

SID, 83	Billy. Jesus Christ, what the hell happened? Look at you! You're fat!
BILLY, 45	I'm not a kid anymore, Sid.
SID, 83	You're not even a human anymore. All that time at sea has turned you into a fucking whale!
BILLY, 45	Okay, Sid. Enough, okay? Nice to see you, too.
SID, 83	Who the hell did this to you?
BILLY, 45	What? No one.
SID, 83	Don't lie to me, Billy. No person in their right mind opens their mouth at the buffet and inhales. Someone did this to you. You were pushed toward the smorgasbord. Who is it?
BILLY, 45	No one did this.
SID, 83	Oh yes they did. There's always someone hiding in those corpulent folds. You're in love!
BILLY, 45	No I'm not.
SID, 83	You are, admit it!
BILLY, 45	No.
SID, 83	Liar.
BILLY, 45	It's Brian! His name is Brian, okay?
SID, 83	Bring him to me!
BILLY, 45	He's not here. He's a civilian, why would he come to a puppet festival?
SID, 83	No, when he could stay at home and bake! Or is his specialty deep frying?
BILLY, 45	It's not his fault. I just gave up. I mean, I'm comfortable. Okay? Okay, Sid?
SID, 83	Fine.
BILLY, 45	Thank you.
SID, 83	You know, it was a puppeteer who invented the Macy's Thanksgiving balloons…

BILLY, 45	Sid!
SID, 83	What? We're at a puppet festival, Billy. We talk trivia, don't we? I thought you'd be interested.
BILLY, 45	What are you doing here?
SID, 83	I beg your pardon? I was coming to these things before you were even born!
BILLY, 45	No, backstage. Why are you here, waiting in the wings?
SID, 83	I'm waiting to go on. Thanks for opening for me, kid.
BILLY, 45	What? You're performing in the gala?
SID, 83	Well, they can hardly celebrate a Century of American Puppetry without me. I'm doing a scene from Shakespeare.
BILLY, 45	With her?
SID, 83	She, sir, is Juliet.
BILLY, 45	I know that, Sid. Why her?
SID, 83	Why not? People know it, people like it.
BILLY, 45	Sid, no. Why not Shylock? Or Prospero? Even Lear. Yes, Lear is perfect for your age.
SID, 83	My age is irrelevant to my interpretation. Art is ageless.
BILLY, 45	But you're not, Sid. Look at you. You're old. You're a little old man and you're going to go on stage and do Juliet. Sid, Juliet is a fourteen-year-old girl. You'll make a fool of yourself. Please, don't embarrass us this way.
SID, 83	Us? After two decades of silence, now you invoke our bond? To spare yourself the association of the very man who taught you how to hold a puppet in your hand? Worried not that mine might tremble or lose my grip, no, nothing so noble as that. Only, perhaps, afraid that even in my present infirmity I will be stronger than you, still.
BILLY, 45	Sid, please. You're great. You always were. They know. I know. But let it go.

SID, 83	No. I'm not done. True, the end has begun. It began without my approval, but I'm still here, so it's not over. It's just the middle, Billy. Maybe the middle of the end, yes, but what would you have me do? Sit down and wait for life to play out? I can't. While I'm still breathing, I will play.
BILLY, 45	You'll die out there.
SID, 83	Then that will be the end. Amen.
	BILLY's theme music is heard in the background. An ANNOUNCER's voice is introducing him.
ANNOUNCER	*(voice-over)* Ladies and gentlemen, Mr. Billy Twinkle and his Stars in Miniature!
SID, 83	You're on, kid. Warm 'em up for the old man, okay?
BILLY, 45	Sid, please…
SID, 83	I wouldn't miss this for the world.
	BILLY and SID are both hung on stage. Lights and background music both fade as we restore to BILLY and handpuppet SID above.
SID	Enough of that. There's no need to see the rest.
BILLY	I'd like to see it.
SID	You were there.
	BILLY removes the onstage marionette of himself.
BILLY	I was on stage, Sid. Come on, let's continue.
SID	Really, Billy, while I'm sure you would derive some perverse pleasure in re-enacting my heart attack, I can assure you there was nothing memorable about it.
BILLY	Sid, you almost died that night.
SID	Which would have been preferable to the reality. No, death merely smirked at me as I fell down… into the waiting arms of that insufferable amateur, Doreen Gray! Do you know she actually had one of her damned Christian sock puppets on her hand when she caught me? Jesus Christ!

BILLY	I'd like to see it.
SID	I'll bet you would.
BILLY	Juliet. I'd like to see it.
SID	I didn't do it, Billy. Remember?
BILLY	Then do it now.

BILLY reaches to the hanging puppets behind him and brings one out into the playing area below. It is a marionette of Juliet. She is identical to the one in the seated SID's hand on stage, although this Juliet is larger and in the same scale as the SID marionette.

SID	Where the hell did you get that?
BILLY	She was back there. Look Sid, she's got that old paddle control you made me use when I was a kid.
SID	That control's a piece of shit.
BILLY	Then why'd you make me use it?
SID	I couldn't have you getting ahead of me too fast.
BILLY	Jesus, Sid! Fine, you hold it.

BILLY gives the control to SID and places the hanging strap over the handpuppet's hand.

SID	Billy, I can't do this.
BILLY	Why not?
SID	Hmmm, let's see. Oh yes, I'm a fucking handpuppet, you asshole, that's why! Grab the leg strings. And keep your mouth shut. Remember, this is my scene.

Light reveals both the marionette playing area and the leaning rail above. The handpuppet SID speaks as Juliet and manipulates the control while BILLY works the leg and arm strings. The marionette of Juliet plays the scene to the lifeless, seated SID marionette on stage.

(as Juliet) "What's here? A cup clos'd in my true love's hand?
Poison, I see, hath been his timeless end.

O churl. Drunk all, and left no friendly drop
To help me after? I will kiss thy lips.
Haply some poison yet doth hang on them
To make me die with a restorative."

Juliet kisses the marionette of SID.

"Thy lips are warm!

"Yea, noise? Then I'll be brief. O happy dagger.
This is thy sheath. There rust, and let me die."

She plunges the dagger into her stomach and dies with her head on SID's lap.

See, Billy? That's the way to do it.

Light fades. Music in, which becomes light and lively, echoing the music from BILLY's first childhood-home flashback. The marionettes of SID and Juliet are removed and hung upstage. The trunk is left in place.

FACE OFF

Lights restore as BRIAN enters. He is BILLY's partner, a nicely maintained man in his mid forties carrying a pampered dog with bulging eyes and an unfortunate underbite. This is Miss de Havilland and she is barking.

BRIAN   I know, baby, I know! It's Daddy!

BILLY enters. He is now forty-seven, and much thinner than the previous flashback. He is wearing casual clothes, specifically a sweater with horizontal stripes.

Welcome home, honey.

They share a lukewarm embrace. The dog barks.

That's right, baby. Daddy's home!

BRIAN speaks in baby voice to BILLY.

	Miss de Havilland says she wants to give you a kiss, Daddy.
BILLY, 47	Oh come on, Brian. She licks her ass.
BRIAN	But she missed her daddy when he was away on the really big boat.

The dog barks again. BRIAN drops the baby voice.

| | Just let her kiss you, Billy. She won't stop barking until you do. |
| BILLY, 47 | Fine. Hello Miss de Havilland. |

BRIAN holds the dog up to BILLY's face.

	Fuck, her breath is foul!
BRIAN	And welcome home to you, too.
BILLY, 47	Sorry. Tough trip.
BRIAN	Well, it couldn't have been all bad. You look fabulous, mister. I see someone's wearing horizontal stripes again!

BILLY crosses to exit.

	Billy, honey, don't go in there.
BILLY, 47	Why not?
BRIAN	It's... different.
BILLY, 47	What's different about the kitchen? Brian?
BRIAN	All of it.
BILLY, 47	What do you mean "all of it"?
BRIAN	We have a new kitchen. Surprise!
BILLY, 47	Why do we have a new kitchen? Brian?
BRIAN	I didn't plan for it, Billy. It just happened.
BILLY, 47	Brian, kitchens don't just happen.
BRIAN	Ours did. And it's not my fault.
BILLY, 47	Then whose fault is it?

BRIAN	Cheryl. She was going to Ikea one day and asked me if I wanted to go with her. Well, I needed another bag of those tea-light candles, so I said sure. And while she was waiting for them to find the missing hardware for her Billy bookcase—which I took as a sign—I just sort of wandered into the kitchen displays.
BILLY, 47	And?
BRIAN	And I bought a new kitchen.
BILLY, 47	Brian, that's what crazy people do! How are we going to pay for a new kitchen?
BRIAN	It's paid for.
BILLY, 47	What? How?
BRIAN	We had all that money in that account.
BILLY, 47	What account? Brian?
BRIAN	You know. The one we don't use. It had sixty-five thousand dollars in it, Billy.
BILLY, 47	That's my face fund!
BRIAN	Your what?
BILLY, 47	My face fund, Brian. To get the work done.
BRIAN	What work?
BILLY, 47	My face! My eyes, my brow, my teeth, all of it.
BRIAN	Billy, that's stupid. You look fine.
BILLY, 47	No, Brian, I look my age!
BRIAN	You are your age, Billy. Why are you being so vain?
BILLY, 47	I'm in show business. I have a necessary level of vanity appropriate to my job.
BRIAN	And now you have a new kitchen.
BILLY, 47	That wasn't your money to spend!
BRIAN	We're a couple, Billy. It's all ours. Not mine. Not yours. Ours.
BILLY, 47	Not my face fund. That's mine!

BRIAN	Fine! Would you rather be single, Billy?
BILLY, 47	I'm in a long-term relationship, Brian. Of course I want to be single! That's all people in long-term relationships dream about!
BRIAN	Well too bad, mister, because you're stuck with me. I happen to love you. You're stuck with Miss de Havilland. She loves you. And you're stuck with a new kitchen, which you are going to love. It's fabulous.

BRIAN exits SR, Miss de Havilland barking noisily at BENJI, age forty-seven, who is standing in the doorway SL. He is still somewhat toothy and freckled, but also oddly sexy. BENJI clears his throat and BILLY turns.

ৎ   ৫

PINOCCHIO'S PYRE

BILLY, 47	Benji? What are you doing here?
BENJI, 47	Hi Billy.
BILLY, 47	Benji, you look great. What happened?
BENJI, 47	Oh, you know: laser surgery, joined a gym, quit smoking, quit drinking, quit puppetry.
BILLY, 47	You what?
BENJI, 47	I quit. I'm not a puppeteer anymore.
BILLY, 47	You can't quit, Benji. We die with a puppet in our hands.
BENJI, 47	I quit, Billy. No big deal.
BILLY, 47	You can't.
BENJI, 47	Why not?
BILLY, 47	Because if you quit, who do I compare myself to?
BENJI, 47	Billy, it's Sid.
BILLY, 47	No, it's not.

BENJI, 47	He fell, Billy. He was doing a show at a festival in the Midwest. When they got him to the hospital, they said his heart was worse than his hip. But he had no insurance, so Doreen Gray took him home and stayed with him.
BILLY, 47	Doreen Gray? Oh my God, Sid always said that Doreen Gray was…
BENJI, 47	He died yesterday, Billy.
BILLY, 47	Oh.
BENJI, 47	He didn't want a funeral or anything.
BILLY, 47	No.
BENJI, 47	And the puppets, Billy. They're gone too.
BILLY, 47	What?
BENJI, 47	Yesterday morning, Doreen went to the store, and that old fucker got out of bed, piled all the puppets in the backyard, and set them on fire.
BILLY, 47	"Give me my robe, put on my crown; I have Immortal longings in me."
	Oh Sid. Stay for dinner, Benj? Brian's in our new kitchen. I'm sure he'd love to see you.
	BENJI hesitates for a moment, then exits toward the kitchen. Light shifts to a tight pool around BILLY. It cross-fades slowly to the leaning rail, where SID and BILLY have been watching.
SID	I thought I might at least have had a partial quotation.
BILLY	What are you talking about?
SID	Well, look at you. Silent as dumbshow. I didn't expect a full eulogy, but could you not even muster a line or two?
BILLY	I was speechless.
SID	Which is why you memorize things to quote. For those moments when you've nothing to say!

BILLY takes the marionette from the playing area and hangs it up backstage.

BILLY I was preoccupied, Sid.

SID Yes, with grief. And guilt.

BILLY Fuck you.

SID Admit it, you were feeling guilty that I had died alone.

BILLY You died with Doreen Gray.

SID That would kill anyone!

BILLY starts down the stairs, followed by SID, and clears the trunk.

BILLY I was angry at you, Sidney. You burned the puppets! You could've left me one puppet!

SID You've got puppets.

BILLY Not yours.

SID How was I to know what you would do with them? Put roller skates on them? Make them do a striptease? Sell them on eBay so your boyfriend could redecorate the bathroom? No. They were my funeral pyre!

BILLY They were beautiful. I wanted them.

SID Then make your own. Hey, I've got an idea! Let's go to a puppet festival!

BILLY No! No more puppet festivals, Sid. Please.

SID It'll be fun!

BILLY You hate puppet festivals.

SID I do not! I went every year.

BILLY But you hated those people.

SID I did not hate them. I just didn't like most of them.

BILLY Then why did you go?

SID They were my family. Which is why you need to go. And there's one happening right now. Hey kid, you're on!

BILLY	Oh no I'm not.
SID	Oh yes you are, Billy. You've still got to do that old man with the bunny ears routine one last time, and then you're going to retire it! And then maybe I can cross into the light without these fucking ears on my head, and you, well, you can do whatever the hell you want.

SID looks out toward the audience.

Oh look. An audience of your peers. Be good, kid, or they'll rip you apart! Hit it!

BILLY's theme music starts and the lighting goes to showbiz state again. BILLY hangs the handpuppet of SID under the stairs, draws the Mylar curtain closed in front of the playing area, grabs a marionette, and hits his pose centre stage while the music flourishes.

BUNNY

The music becomes the underscore for BUNNY. He is a caricature of an elderly man, wearing a blue hospital gown, a tattered bathrobe, and bedroom slippers. For no apparent reason other than the visual absurdity of it, he has a pair of pink fabric bunny ears on his head. They are identical to the ones worn by the SID handpuppet. There is a length of surgical tubing running from BUNNY's back/bum, which runs up to the control in BILLY's hand.

BUNNY shuffles very slowly to the front of the puppet stage, where he smiles at the audience. He looks over the edge onto the main floor and does an elaborate windup in preparation to jump off. BILLY taps BUNNY on the shoulder, pointing to the SR stairs. BUNNY shuffles to them, stands on the stair closest to the puppet stage level, and looks down.

BUNNY	Help.

He hops down the next two stairs.

Hop. Hop.

BUNNY shuffles to CS.

I'm Bunny. That's my name. See?

He touches his bunny ears.

I like balloons.

He shuffles toward the edge of the stage.

Do you like balloons?

Would you like to see my balloon?

It's a nice pink one. See?

He lifts his hospital gown and reveals a balloon jutting out from his droopy underwear.

Would you like to blow it… up?

BILLY offers the end of the tube to someone in the front row.

I already stretched it out.

BILLY blows into the tube and the balloon starts to inflate.

If you twist it you can make an animal. Or a hat.

BUNNY shuffles along the stage and, seeing a woman, stops there.

You're pretty.

The balloon inflates a bit more. He shuffles CS as his balloon deflates. He stops and looks down.

Houston, we have a problem!

He shuffles to SL and looks at another woman in the front row.

You're the wind beneath my wings.

BUNNY blinks and shuffles quickly away. The balloon grows bigger until BUNNY starts to float, lifted off the ground by the big pink balloon sticking out of his shorts.

Up, up, and away!

> *BILLY spins him round and round as the balloon slowly deflates and BUNNY lands on the ground with a gentle thud. He sits on the ground and looks up to BILLY.*

I want to go home.

> *BUNNY stands. He turns upstage and starts to shuffle off as light fades and the number ends. BILLY puts BUNNY away, climbs the stairs, and opens the Mylar curtains. Light restores on both the marionette playing area and the bridge above.*

BACK TO THE FLOCK

BILLY   Okay Sid, that's it. Sid? Sid, I won't do Bunny anymore, okay? Sid? Sid, where are you?

> *DOREEN Gray enters. She is a plump older woman, wearing a T-shirt on which is printed "I Heart Puppets." On one hand she holds a miniature Muppet-like puppet. It is green with a full yarn beard and hair. The puppet is unclothed and affixed to a wooden cross, the little fleece hands literally nailed in position.*

DOREEN   Hey there. Billy! I'm so glad to see you!

BILLY   Doreen Gray?! Can you?

DOREEN   Can I what, dear?

BILLY   See me.

DOREEN   Clear as day, and I'm better for it. You're a sight for sore eyes!

BILLY   How?

DOREEN   Well, you haven't changed that much over the years, Billy Ruggles! You've still got that twinkle in your eye like you did when you were a little boy.

BILLY   Doreen, how can you see me? I'm not a puppet.

DOREEN	Well of course you're not. You're a person. And you know why, Billy?
BILLY	Uh… I don't know.
DOREEN	Oh you do too! Come on, Billy, it's inside your heart.
BILLY	Uh, because the Blue Fairy brought me back to Geppetto and turned me into a real live boy?
DOREEN	Oh silly Billy! No. It's because Jesus gave his life so you could have yours. Isn't that right, Jesus?

DOREEN lifts the puppet of JESUS up and converses with it. The mouth of the puppet moves when it speaks, although the lip-synch is dreadful.

JESUS	Uh, that's right, Doreen.
DOREEN	Jesus, look who it is. The prodigal son has returned!
JESUS	Hey there, Billy!

BILLY does not respond.

DOREEN	I don't think he can hear you, Jesus.
JESUS	Hey there, Billy!
BILLY	Uh, yeah, hey… Jesus.

DOREEN stops her puppeteering.

DOREEN	I'm glad you came to this festival, Billy. Mr. Diamond would have liked that.
BILLY	I heard you were nice to him. Thanks, Doreen.
DOREEN	It was my pleasure, Billy. He was a wonderful man.
BILLY	Doreen, Sid could be pretty awful.
DOREEN	I never took it personally. I can't imagine what it was like for him; all those magnificent voices in his head, all that talent in his hands, all those experiences inside him. Oh, I wasn't good enough to get as close as you, but I'm surely grateful to have gotten as close as I did.
BILLY	I didn't get as close as you think.
DOREEN	Billy, you were his son! That's what he told me.

BILLY	When?
DOREEN	That final morning. Right before he barbequed the puppets.
BILLY	He was mad at me, Doreen.
DOREEN	No he wasn't. You were mad at him. You know what he said to me, Billy? He said, "Doreen, you insufferable mitten-wiggling charlatan"—he always used such fancy words, you know—he said, "There's a tempest brewing in that boy, and I'll just have to weather the storm." He knew why you were away, Billy, but he never gave up hope that you'd come home.
BILLY	But I didn't, Doreen. I never said goodbye.
DOREEN	You don't have to. Isn't that right, Jesus?
	DOREEN lifts the puppet of JESUS up again.
JESUS	That's right, Doreen. My Kingdom is eternal.
DOREEN	Jesus, is that why you're bleeding up there on that cross?

JESUS	So you and Billy can live forever.
DOREEN	Well shoot, Jesus, that's awfully nice of you. Why would you do that for little old me and Billy up there?
JESUS	Because I love you, Doreen.
DOREEN	And Billy, too?
JESUS	More than he knows. I love you, Billy.
DOREEN	Did you hear that, Billy? Jesus loves you!
JESUS	I love you, Billy. I love you, Billy!
BILLY	Okay, yeah. Thanks. Thank you, Jesus.

DOREEN lowers the puppet.

DOREEN	I do that bit in my act, you know, have Jesus talk with the audience and all. I think it helps the children have a personal relationship with him. Say, Billy, would you like to see my act?
BILLY	Oh God, no. I mean, Jesus is great, Doreen. You've really nailed him.
DOREEN	It would mean the world to me if you would critique my act, Billy. I did my act every day for Mr. Diamond while I was with him, but he was just speechless, poor old fella. I did see tears in his eyes, so I think it touched his heart, what was left of it.
BILLY	I couldn't bear it, Doreen. Having you go to all that trouble.
DOREEN	Oh shoot, Billy, it's no trouble. Hit my groove track on the boom box, Billy.

BILLY looks down at his feet and finds a miniature boom box. He lifts it to the leaning rail, presses a button, and a thumping hip-hop track begins. DOREEN and JESUS move to the music, and she begins to rap.

Now let me introduce you to the man from Galilee
His name is Jesus Christ and he died for you and me
He's drippin' blood from head to toe but don't y'all be sad

He's come to give the Word up, yo,
So you'd best not be bad.

Word. Word of Jesus Christ
Word. Word of Jesus Christ

So listen dogs, and listen cats, and listen all you kids
Jesus has a message, your attention now he bids
Every time you lie or steal you nail him through the heart
Jesus needs a bandage, dude,
Now won't you do your part?

Word. Word of Jesus Christ
Word. Word of Jesus Christ

He wants you for his homey, he needs you in his crew
His crib is really famous and there's room for me and you
Don't be a drive-by phoney, bro; walk with Him instead
Take the hand of Jesus, yo,
And raise him from the dead.

Word. Word of Jesus Christ.
Word up. Word of Jesus Christ.
Peace out. Word of Jesus Christ.
Amen.

It's original material.

BILLY	Doreen… why do you do it?
DOREEN	It makes me happy.
BILLY	But… you're not very good.
DOREEN	I know. I suck! But even so, it makes me feel better. People laugh at me, Billy, I know that. But no one can doubt that I believe.
BILLY	In what, Doreen?
DOREEN	Tomorrow, and tomorrow, and tomorrow.
BILLY	You're a piece of work, Doreen Gray.

DOREEN	I'm a piece of work in progress, Billy. So I have to keep on moving, because in ten minutes there's a workshop on flocking foam-rubber puppet heads with dryer lint and I can't miss it, even though I'll probably suck at that too.
	DOREEN gathers herself and starts off.
BILLY	Flock on, Doreen.
	She stops and turns, looking up at BILLY.
DOREEN	Billy, don't leave us again, y'hear?
	She holds up her puppet again.
JESUS	Weather the storm.
	She exits.
BILLY	Sid, you can come out now, she's gone. Sid? Sidney.
	BILLY goes down the stairs and continues looking for SID.
	Sid, stop this. Don't be pissed, okay? Sid, come on, let's not leave it this way. Not this time.
	Subtly and through the course of the following scene, the lighting becomes nighttime again, as it was when BILLY tried to jump ship.

ROCKET LAUNCH

BILLY looks under the stairs where he had last hung the SID handpuppet, but instead takes another marionette in his hand there. It is short-strung like BILLY's variety marionettes, enabling him to manipulate it on the deck. But this marionette is not from his act. Before it is seen, BILLY backs away from the stairs.

BILLY	Whoa. I'm not ready for this.
	ROCKET enters in BILLY's hand. He is a slight teenage boy of fifteen, otherworldly in his beauty,

> *and very androgynous. ROCKET is dressed in
> an odd getup of black tights, a black, cropped long-
> sleeved T-shirt, and a pair of blue-black angel wings
> on his back, which have sequins sewn amongst the
> feathers. In one hand he holds a smaller marionette
> of a muscular man, naked save for a G-string and
> red stilettos.*

I looked back, right? That was the point, wasn't it?
So I get it now. You can go, but I'm not going with you.
Leave me alone.

ROCKET I just want to talk to you.

BILLY Oh God. Where are you from? Heaven, or hell?

ROCKET I'm from Middle Earth.

BILLY What?

ROCKET Middle Earth. You know? Mythology? The home
of humankind? Halfway between Asgard and the
underworld?

BILLY You're a troll?

ROCKET You should talk.

BILLY What? Who the fuck are you?

ROCKET I'm Rocket.

BILLY You're just a kid!

ROCKET I'm fifteen!

BILLY No, I mean, you're not the Angel of Death?

ROCKET Are you drunk? My dad says showbiz people are
drunks.

BILLY No, I'm not drunk. What are you doing here?

ROCKET We got on in Miami, remember? Probably not, 'cause
you're drunk.

BILLY I'm not drunk!

ROCKET	I wouldn't blame you. I mean, being fired and all. But I loved when you shushed that woman in the audience. She was a pig.
BILLY	Watch your mouth.
ROCKET	That's what you called her.

BILLY	I did not.
ROCKET	You did so. When you were praying.
BILLY	You saw that?
ROCKET	I wanted to show you my puppet before you killed yourself.
BILLY	Well I'm not going to kill myself, okay?
ROCKET	Why not?
BILLY	I changed my mind.
ROCKET	Good, 'cause I need your help.
BILLY	Why should I help you?
ROCKET	Because I'm the next one. I'm going to do it anyway, and you could save me a lot of time if you just helped me.
BILLY	With what?
ROCKET	This. It's a stripper.
BILLY	It's a man.
ROCKET	It's a tranny.
BILLY	What?
ROCKET	You know, a man who dresses up like a woman.

       He sings.

       It's Manny the Tranny
       A little bit he, a little bit she
       He's wearing a heel
       But the package is real…

BILLY	Whoa, whoa, whoa! How old did you say you were?
ROCKET	Fifteen.
BILLY	And you've got a transvestite stripper puppet?
ROCKET	Yeah. That's why I need your help. I can get the clothes to come off, that's easy.
BILLY	No it's not.

ROCKET	You do it. I want my stripper to put the clothes back on!
BILLY	Can't be done.
ROCKET	Why not?
BILLY	Because, no one has ever done that.
ROCKET	That's why you have to help me figure it out.
BILLY	Look, I can't. Not right now.
ROCKET	I know. I just wanted to meet you. That's why my parents brought me on this stupid cruise. We'll figure it out at Easter, okay? I get two weeks off school, so I'll come stay with you.
BILLY	Ah, I don't think so.
ROCKET	Brian said it was okay.
BILLY	You talked to Brian?
ROCKET	Yeah, when I phoned. He seemed real excited.
BILLY	And he said you could come at Easter?
ROCKET	Yeah. He's gonna renovate the guest room for me.
	BILLY is momentarily speechless. He composes himself.
BILLY	We'll discuss this with your parents, okay?
ROCKET	Okay. Just don't be drunk when you meet my dad.
BILLY	I'm not drunk!
	ROCKET starts to leave.
	Hey kid. What did you say your name was?
ROCKET	Rocket. It's really Kevin, but I like Rocket better.
BILLY	Well, Rocket… I'd lose the wings if I were you.
ROCKET	I like them. They're sparkly.
	ROCKET exits and is hung under the stairs. Music in, very softly. BILLY stands there for a moment, shaking his head.

BILLY   My God, Sid… can you believe that kid?

> *We hear BILLY's "twinkly" theme again. BILLY looks around for SID, but instead finds a pair of pink fabric bunny ears on a headband, identical to those worn by the SID handpuppet. BILLY looks at them, slowly brings them close to his face, and kisses them.*
>
> *He walks downstage near the edge of the deck.*

I think I owe you that eulogy, Sidney.

> *BILLY puts the bunny ears on his head and kneels.*

"Now my charms are all o'erthrown,
And what strength I have's mine own,
Which is most faint: now, 'tis true,
I must be here confined by you,
Or sent to Naples. Let me not,
Since I have my dukedom got,
And pardoned the deceiver, dwell
In this bare island by your spell;"

> *Music in: a beautiful horn choir arrangement of SID's theme.*

"But release me from my bands
With the help of your good hands:
Gentle breath of yours my sails
Must fill, or else my project fails,
Which was to please. Now I want
Spirits to enforce, Art to enchant;
And my ending is despair,
Unless I be relieved by prayer,
Which pierces so, that it assaults
Mercy itself, and frees all faults.
As you from crimes would pardoned be,
Let your indulgence set me free."

> *BILLY stands as lighting changes to dawn.*

A *Tempest* brewing in me…

> *He runs up the stairs to the centre bridge. BILLY looks into the horizon and smiles.*

Land, ho!

Music resolves as lights fade to black.

The end.

photo by Trudie Lee

RONNIE BURKETT has been captivated by puppetry since the age of seven, when he opened the World Book Encyclopedia to "Puppets." He began touring his puppet shows at the age of fourteen and has been on the road ever since.

Recognized as one of Canada's foremost theatre artists, Ronnie Burkett has been credited with creating some of the world's most elaborate and provocative puppetry. Ronnie Burkett Theatre of Marionettes was formed in 1986 and has stimulated an unprecedented adult audience for puppet theatre, continuously playing to great critical and public acclaim on Canada's major stages and as a guest company at international theatre festivals.

Ronnie has received numerous awards in the Canadian theatre as a playwright, actor, and designer for his work with Theatre of Marionettes, and international recognition including a Village Voice OBIE Award in New York for off-Broadway Theatre and four Citations of Excellence in the Art of Puppetry from the American Center of the Union Internationale de la Marionnette. *Billy Twinkle* is the eleventh production from Theatre of Marionettes, and follows the now-retired international successes *10 Days on Earth*, *Provenance*, and the Memory Dress Trilogy of *Tinka's New Dress*, *Street of Blood*, and *Happy*.

When not touring, Ronnie can be found surrounded by more than 1,200 books on puppetry, two dogs, Plasticine, and woodworking tools in his Toronto studio, where he is creating yet another new show.